Lady Marys Book of Receipts

Recipes, Remedies and Cures from An Irish Georgian House

Sally Clements

Dedication

For Davy, Holly, Jenny & Charlie and in memory of Sam.

Lady Mary's Book of Receipts

Copyright © Sally Clements, 2021

All rights reserved. No part of
this book may be reproduced
or used in any manner
without written permission of
the copyright owner except
for the use of quotations
in a book review. For more
information, address:
sally@sallyclements.com

First edition February 2021

ISBN 979-8-7072-91531- (hardback)

CONTENTS

- **DEDICATION** 6
- **PREFACE** 8
- **INTRODUCTION** 15
- **CURES** 31
- **FOOD AND DRINK** 103
- **HOUSEHOLD** 171
- **ACKNOWLEDGEMENTS** 213

PREFACE

PREFACE

Killadoon in Celbridge, Co. Kildare, Ireland was the family home of the Clements family from 1765-2019. I moved to Killadoon in 1991 with my husband, Charlie. We shared the house with two elderly cousins who had lived here all their lives, and over the next twenty-eight years we brought up our family there.

The house was home to a comprehensive archive of books, papers, and artifacts of all types. Built between 1765 and 1770 for Robert Clements, it was inherited by his son, Nathaniel who married Mary Bermingham–the Lady Mary of this book's title, in the early 1800s.

The house was a treasure trove of original fabric, linen,

wallpaper, art, books and porcelain collected and owned by the Earl and Countess. The drawing room wallpaper dates from the 1820s. The previous lady of the house remembered seeing it being cleaned with white bread, probably around 1910.

I found Lady Mary's book of receipts in the drawing room not long after we moved in, and it sparked my interest. Squinting at her handwriting, I knew right away that I had discovered something special. The book dates from around 1820, and at that time in Ireland it was usual for ladies in the large country houses to compile books of recipes and cures, often described as books of receipts. The notebook is full of food recipes and wonderful remedies and concoctions from the period, some of which have stood the test of time and some of which have been proven to be downright dangerous!

Equally fascinating is the collection of letters tucked into the front cover. These show who the recipes, remedies and cures were actually sent by, and further examination provides an insight into the society in which she lived, and the problems endemic in the country at the time. They were sent not only by family and friends who lived on other nearby large country estates, but also by soldiers, doctors and politicians.

ABOVE:
A PAPERCUT SILHOUETTE FROM THE KILLADOON COLLECTION

OPPOSITE PAGE:
DETAIL OF AN OLD PAINTING OF KILLADOON

So this book has recipes, but is not a cookbook. Has cures, but many of ingredients used are deadly and dangerous today. Even basic health standards have changed much in two-hundred years, so all of the receipts should be carefully assessed before making, and it is probably safest to look rather than make!

Each recipe had something interesting about it. Either the person who sent it, an unusual ingredient, or some other social history element. The illustrations are mostly from fabrics/wallpapers/drawings in Lady Mary's collection.

INTRODUCTION

Lady Mary's Book of Recipes and Remedies was written by Mary Clements, 2nd Lady Leitrim, who became chatelaine of Killadoon in 1804, and lived there until her death in 1840.

She married Nathaniel Clements at the tender age of twenty-one to his thirty-two, and a wealth of letters between them reveals that they were devoted to each other, and their children. To fully understand the lady, however, it's interesting to look back at her life before she married.

Mary Bermingham, as she was then, born the eldest of two daughters of William Bermingham of Rosshill in Galway. Her younger sister, Anne, became the Countess of Charlemont on her marriage.

PREVIOUS PAGE:
PORTRAIT OF MARY BERMINGHAM BY THOMAS SULLY
REPRODUCED BY PERMISSION OF THE SKINNER GALLERY

SKETCHES FROM LADY MARY'S SKETCHBOOK

15

The estate of Rosshill was a very large one, conferring the status of heiress on both daughters. Rosshill was a beautiful home, standing on the shores of Lough Mask. But its isolation meant that it was also a dangerous one.

Both of the Bermingham (sometimes also written as Birmingham) sisters were great beauties, and at that time the abduction of heiresses was popular with Irish bachelors, who would draw up lists of eligible heiresses and kidnap them, forcing them into marriage as a way of improving their own circumstances. These were the 'abduction clubs', where the members would carry off rich heiresses. Armed men wearing masks, would surround a house in the dead of night, carry away the heiresses, threatening anyone who tried to intervene, and forcibly marry them before the law could prevent it.

These abduction clubs were a very real danger to the Bermingham heiresses, and William Bermingham, a cultured man with a keen interest in art and literature, decided to move with his family to Italy, in order to protect his daughters from abduction, and also give them the opportunity to enhance their education.

Mary and her younger sister Anne featured in a book written in 1907 by Wilmott Wilmott-Dixon's entitled, Queens of Beauty and their romances Vol II, which was a testament to the great beauties of the previous century. In it, the author talks of Mary's first season in 1796. She was eighteen, and by all accounts, captivating.

Here's an extract:
Florence was then even more popular than Rome among the English residents in Italy, and the season of 1796, in which the Berminghams made their first appearance there, was more than usually brilliant. Among the leaders of Florentine society Louise Comtesse d'Albanie, widow of Charles Edward Stuart, " The Young Pretender," still held a high place, despite the scandal of her relations with Vittorio Alfieri, and she was at once captivated by the beauty and naivete of Mary Bermingham, the elder of the two sisters. To have won the favour of the Queen of that select coterie was, of course, an immediate passport to recognition, and Mary was at once installed as the acknowledged " belle of the season." But there

ABOVE:
SKETCH FROM LADY MARY'S SKETCHBOOK

OPPOSITE:
ANNE BERMINGHAM PAINTED BY
FRANÇOIS-XAVIER FABRE IN 1796. THIS
PAINTING WAS COPIED BY QUEEN LOUISE,
AND HUNG IN THE LIBRARY OF PALAZZO
GIANFIGLIAZZI IN FLORENCE.
@MUSÉE FABRE DE MONTPELLIER AGGLO-
MÉRATION - PHOTOGRAPH BY FRÉDÉRIC
JAULMES

were many who thought that they saw in the younger sister, Anne, who was not yet " out," the dawning of a beauty which would eclipse Mary's. Both girls had something of the artist temperament. Mary could paint fairly well — enough to draw fervid expressions of eulogy from the admirers of her beauty. Anne had the gift of reeling off pretty, if rather watery, verses, and at first there was a freshness and simplicity about the two Irish girls, with their fascinating Irish eyes, and their bewitching Galway brogue, that took every one by storm.

OPPOSITE:
PORTRAIT OF LADY COWPER

Extracts from Mary's letters were published in a book entitled "Some fair Hibernians – being a supplementary volume to "Some celebrated Irish Beauties of the last century." (1897) by Frances A Gerard.

She writes of a ball she attended, during the season in Florence. *"They are all bent upon being kind to us," writes Mary Birmingham to a friend. "Lady Cowper dressed me last Saturday for a ball at the Casino, where I went with Madame d'Albani. Lady Webster and Lord Holland came, I bored myself extremely at the ball, and wherever I go I am always bored since I have been at Florence." And then she confesses with adorable candour that she is always so — "when I am not quiet: it is constitutional, so do not scold me. And as for being an old maid, do not speak against that brilliant state, for certain it will be mine as the only one I deserve." In the next paragraph she goes on to describe her dress, and considering her depressed state of mind, she takes a natural and very feminine satisfaction in dwelling on such adornment. "I must, however, tell you about my dress on Saturday, for it was almost entirely the work of Lady Cowper. On my head I had a long roll of crape turned round and round, and between my hair two feathers of half a league of height, with an esprit between them ; sleeves of white satin (this is the fashion with all sorts of dresses) ; a body of purple satin with little sleeves of the same, and a purple fringe which hung on the white satin ; waist very short, and the petticoat of plain muslin; the belt a narrow white satin ribbon with a rosette behind. This is detail enough."*

All of these extracts paint a vivid picture of Mary in her late teens. The people that she befriended during her stay in Italy, and later in Germany, London and Dublin would in later years send her recipes for food, drink, and all the household concoctions and medicines that a lady needed for the running of her home.
In late 1796, the family attended the German court in Carlsbad, where Mary was much taken by Prince August of Saxe-Gotha.

She writes:
"Wednesday we were presented at the reception. I was never more astonished than with several things that occurred. In the first place we entered — my mother and I — and the Baron Schimananski (one of our Poles). We passed quietly into another room, where the sister of the Duchess of Kurland, with a suite of twenty ladies, besieged us from behind, so we had to face round and be presented, one after another. As they were all married, I took no part, but my turn came. From the other end fifty young ladies came and made me curtseys, and overpowered me with English, which they all talked. Really, at the end of quarter of an hour, with all the noise, my senses had departed, and I did not know whether I was standing on my head or my heels.
In the end a young person arrived whom every one kissed, and whom every one hastened to present to me as one who talked English. But she was very different from the crowd I had seen hitherto. She was as beautiful as an

angel, and really spoke English well. We began talking to each other, and the evening passed very agreeably. But this was not all. We were in the midst of a circle of one hundred persons, young men and young women, when all of a sudden a signal was given, and every one ran to the other side of the salle with all their strength. You may judge how this ruse seized me with astonishment, and I remained stupefied. I thought the house had taken fire. It was only a few cups of chocolate that had caused all this fracas.

Only for my charming Countess Clare, I should have remained standing in the middle of this enormous salon without a living being within a hundred steps of me. I assure you my knees ache with all the curtseys I had to make that night. Amongst the people there were some very nice and very elegant. Madame de Rodenham, her daughters, and

BELOW:
LUDWIG DÖLL, PUBLIC DOMAIN, VIA WIKIMEDIA COMMONS. HERZOG AUGUST VON SACHSEN-GOTHA-ALTENBURG. (GRANDFATHER TO PRINCE ALBERT).

23

Countess Clare, and, above all, the Prince of Saxe-Gotha was very
agreeable. The eldest of the princesses, who is beautiful, is in love, they say,
with the Prince of Saxe-Gotha. His father sent him here expressly to make
up to her; but he doesn't care for her, and she is so used to be sought out and
almost adored by many princes that she is quite piqued by the coldness of
this one.

We are to be presented to them at the ball on Sunday or Monday, and my
mother is to go to the duchess. You know, or do you not know, that the
Duke of Kurland is no longer a sovereign prince ; for, seeing the ability of
the Empress of Russia, seeing the fate of the King of Poland, trembling for
himself, he sold his estates a year ago to the empress; he is now enormously
rich, but no longer a sovereign. He has no son, therefore it is just as well.
The gaiety of the Germans is astonishing. You can imagine how it strikes a
person who has lived so long in quiet Italy, and who at the age of nineteen
is almost an old woman. I am quite delighted to do my apprenticeship
before returning to Ireland, where the young ladies are almost as youthful as
here."

Before closing this letter, she gives her correspondent an account of the ball
given by the Duchess of Kurland, and from the tone of ill-concealed elation
in the letter, it is evident she had been much admired — especially by the
Prince of Saxe-Gotha — and enjoyed her triumph as much as so blighted
a young being could, evidently forgetful of the fact that she was "almost an
old woman."

"I have just returned from the ball, my dear. I danced all the possible,
except waltzes, which are not in the least bon ton or comme il faut, I have

had more partners than I wanted, and am engaged tonight till the fourth with excellent partners, the Prince of Saxe-Gotha amongst others. He is devoted to dancing. ... And by-the-bye, I want to tell you a little story that the young Count Slam told me yesterday. His father was great friends with Lord Gilford, just when this one left Ireland; they were at Milan, where Lord Gilford bored himself to death. Count Slam said to him, — But, my friend, let us try Vienna; perhaps that'll please you better.' 'Oh no,' said the other, I have a horror of Vienna ; I'll never go there.' After repeating very often this thing, he said, 'To satisfy you, I'll go there for ten days. 1 leave everything behind me here.'

He went to Vienna, spent three months there without leaving it, and married Mdlle. de.

Predestination, my dear! It will be for you one day. I am going to the ball, but 1 should almost prefer to die than to be always in society; there is nothing which so tires the heart, the spirit, and the soul."

At the end of 1797, William brought his family back to Ireland, unfortunately on the eve of the great rebellion. They lived in Dublin, as the turmoil in the country made return to Galway impossible. During this time Rosshill was gutted and burned, totally destroyed by rebels.

BELOW:
SKETCH FROM LADY MARY'S SKETCHBOOK

The season of 1799 took place in a joyful atmosphere borne of the relief that at last, the rebellion was over. The gentry in their Dublin houses vied with each other to provide impressive evenings of entertainment.

Some fair Hibernians records:

The Miss Birminghams, for Anne was now a fully-fledged young lady, were the belles of the Dublin season of 1799. Since the days of the Gunnings, no greater beauties had appeared, and, as Horace Walpole had said of the first-named, the fact that they were two equally handsome increased the effect, for, taken singly, there were many women quite as beautiful. "I never saw two such beautiful creatures as the Birminghams," writes Lady Morgan; "the youngest the loveliest of the two." This would appear to have been the universal opinion. Mary, however, had special charms of her own. She was full of esprit, as we have seen by her correspondence, with a true artistic nature, as was evidenced by her fitful moods.

She was engaged, before the end of this season of 1799, to the eldest son of Lord Leitrim, and was married to him early in 1800. There is little heard of her after this. We have glimpses of her occasionally, but her name was not so well known in the world of fashion, both at home and abroad, as that of Anne, who, in 1802, when she was barely twenty, became the wife of Francis William, second Earl of Charlemont, who had succeeded his father in 1799.

So Mary, aged twenty-one married Nathaniel Clements, honeymooned at Killadoon, and in 1804, became its mistress.

BELOW:
SKETCH FROM LADY MARY'S SKETCHBOOK

CURES

In this section on cures the text of the cure is faithfully reproduced from the original—spelling and all.

Many of these cures are dangerous today, so are included for interest's sake, rather than for use!

Three Cures for Chilblains
First Cure

The first receipt for chilblains has alum as an ingredient. Alum is potassium aluminium sulphate or an ammonium aluminum sulfate. In its natural form, alum has been used for more than two thousand years, and is still used in some medical preparations, often as an astringent to stop bleeding. The styptic pencil used to heal shaving nicks, for example, is made from moulded alum. It can also be found in some toothpastes as it is effective for removing bacteria, and it is sold in its crystal form as a deodorant, because of its antibacterial qualities.

A lump of alum about the size of a large yolk of an egg, put into half a pint of cold water and left to dissolve perfectly; when wanted for use to be warmed, and the part affected to be well rubbed with it at night, and then wrapped in flannel or a worsted sock or stocking put on –

Sir Walter Farquhar's Receipt for Chilblains

This recipe for chilblains was given by Sir Walter Farquhar. Farquhar established an apothecary shop in Great Marlborough Street in London in 1769, and later became the physician of the Prince of Wales and the English prime minister William Pitt the Younger.

His recipe uses camphorated oil, which is made by distilling oil from a camphor tree. Camphorated oil has long been used as an effective treatment for sprains and muscle ache due to its analgesic and anti-inflammatory properties, although it is less popular today, as large doses are known to be toxic.

The second ingredient, extract of Saturn, was a lead-based formulation developed in the early 1770s by the French surgeon Thomas Goulard. At the time, lead in suspension was considered an excellent solution for all manner of inflammations, and was also an effective astringent. Extract of Saturn was abandoned as an ingredient because it could cause lead poisoning, and because better, safer products became available.

Mix two tablespoons of camphorated oil with one tablespoonful of Extract of Saturn, and rub the part affected twice a day -not to be used after the chilblains are burst, except round the edges of them.

ABOVE:
HENRY RAEBURN, PUBLIC DOMAIN, VIA WIKIMEDIA COMMONS
SIR WALTER FARQUHAR, 1ST BT, (1738-1819), BY SIR HENRY RAEBURN. PAINTED C.1790

Lady Sydney's cure for Chilblains

The final cure for chilblains, from Lady Sydney, seems the most benign of the three. The author of this recipe could be either Mary's sister-in-law, Caroline, who married John Thomas Townsend, 2nd Viscount Sydney, in 1802 and died giving birth to her first son in 1805, or a friend of Mary's, Lady Sydney Morgan, one of the most famous early female Irish novelists. From humble beginnings Lady Sydney rose to fame because of her popular novels, most notably The Wild Irish Girl, published in 1806.

In Lady Sydney Morgan's memoirs she mentions meeting Mary and Nathaniel in Rome in 1820. She detailed a visit to Rome by the newly crowned Queen Caroline, who was married to George IV, and had become Queen on the death of George III in January of that year.

We have Queen Caroline here. At first this made a great fuss whether she was or was not to be visited by her subjects, when lo! she refused to see any of them, and leads the most perfectly retired life! We met her one day driving out in a state truly royal; I never saw her so splendid. Young Austen followed in an open carriage; he is an interesting-looking young man. She happened to arrive at an inn near Rome, when Lord and Lady Leitrim were there; she sent for them and invited them to tea. Lady Leitrim told me her manner was perfect, and altogether she was a most improved woman; the Baron attended her at tea, but merely as a chamberlain, and was not introduced.

The spirits of wine referred to here is actually brandy. In a book called *Cyclopaedia, or an Universal Dictionary of Arts and Sciences*, published in 1728, the following method was described for distilling brandy:

A cucurbit was filled half full of the liquor from which brandy was to be drawn and then raised with a little fire until about one sixth part was distilled, or until that which falls into the receiver was entirely flammable. This liquor, distilled only once, was called spirit of wine or brandy.

The sweet oil used in this recipe is most likely unpurified olive oil, a popular ingredient in medicinal remedies for thousands of years.

Half a pint of spirits of wine, half a teacup full of sweet oil, a lump of camphor, the size of a walnut – mix all well together and rub the chilblains several times a day.

OPPOSITE:
LADY CAROLINE, VISCOUNTESS SYDNEY, BY SIR THOMAS LAWRENCE.

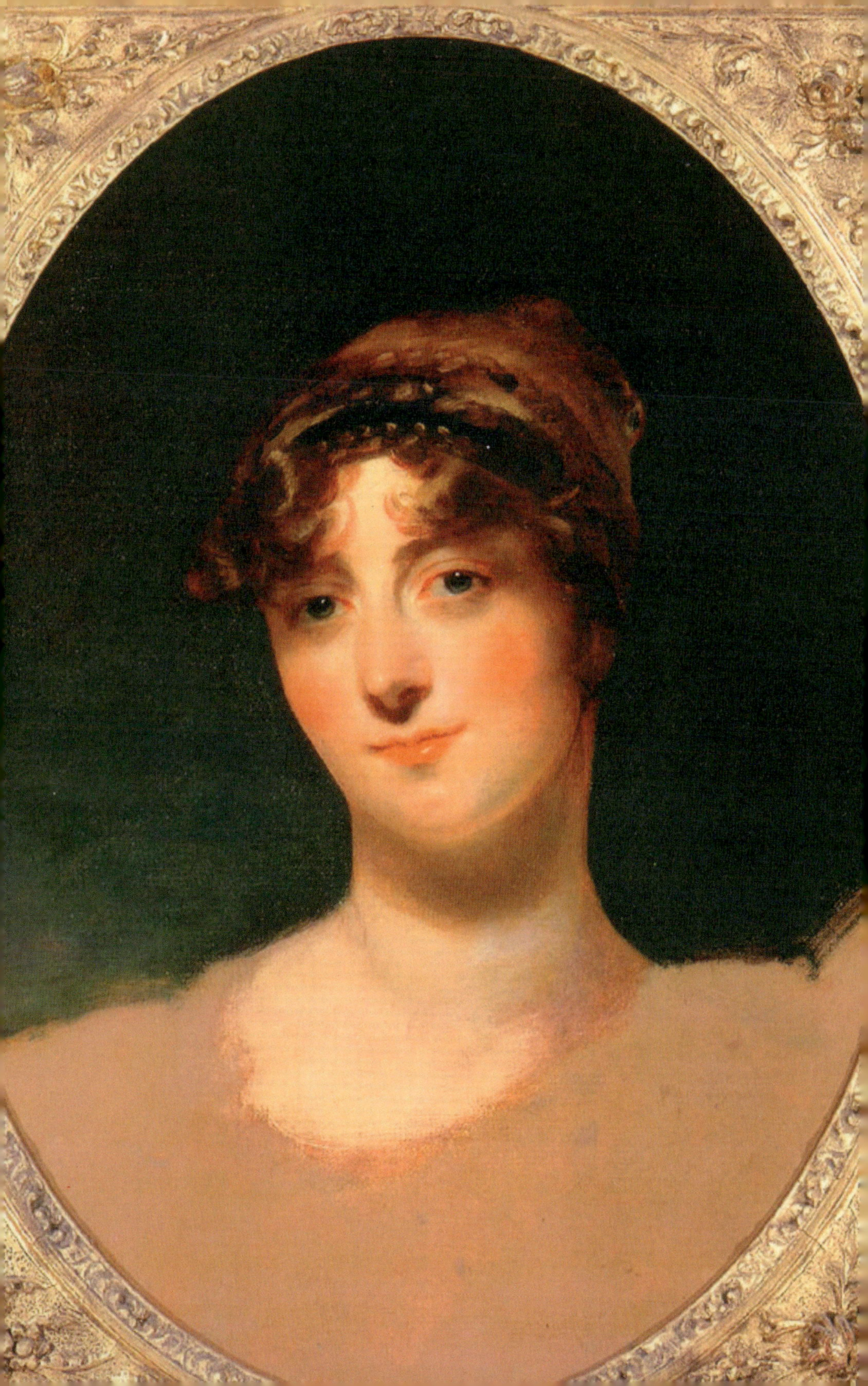

Red gargle for a sore throat

Borax is sodium borate, a boron compound imported to Arabia via the Silk Road from dry lake beds in Tibet until 1890. It is a white powder, and its crystals dissolve easily in water. Today it is often used in cleaning and laundry products, as well as in the making of china. It has been proven to be a carcinogen when consumed in large quantities over five to ten years.

Bole Armoniac is a red clay that comes from Armenia. It is an astringent, and was prescribed for haemorrhage and diarrhoea. It is also used as a colouring agent for bookbinding. It can be found today used by gilders doing water gilding, or gilding on bole, where loose sheets of gold are applied onto a layer of bole.

Take the size of a nutmeg of rock alum, the same quantity of borax, and double the quantity of Bole Armoniac, pound them into a very fine powder; then take half a pint of Honey and a quarter of a pint of vinegar, boil them all together till it becomes pretty thick, mixing them well. Gargle the throat with the above frequently.

Cool cream from Lady Hinchingbrooke

Lady Hinchingbrooke was married to George Montagu, 6th Earl of Sandwich. Her name before her marriage was Lady Louisa Mary Anne Julia Harriet Lowry-Corry, and she was the daughter of the 1st Earl of Belmore and Lady Harriet Hobart, daughter of the 2nd Earl of Buckinghamshire, The Lord Lieutenant of Ireland. Her daughter, Lady Caroline Montagu, married Count Alexander Walewski, son of Napoleon Bonaparte, Emperor of France.

Thomas Carlyle wrote to his mother on 3 September 1848: *Lady Sandwich used to live always in Paris, till she was driven hence by the late Revolutions: a brisk talking, friendly and rather entertaining character,—has been very beautiful at one time; she has no other daughter left but this, and no Son but one: plenty of money, and fair health &c, but alas, nothing to do…*

In the ingredient list is virgin's wax, which is new, white beeswax. Spermaceti is a wax that it found inside the head cavity of the sperm whale. It was widely available in the 1800s, and was used in cosmetics and candle making. A good alternative today is jojoba oil, which can be substituted in this recipe.

4 ounces of oil of sweet almonds, half an ounce of virgin's wax, quarter of an ounce of spermaceti. Take the above things, put them into a saucepan till all are melted, then pour in rose water, stirring it all the time. Throw off the first water, and put more on – you will then find it quite white. NB. Cold cream must be kept constantly swimming in rose water.

OPPOSITE:
LOUISA MONTAGU, VISCOUNTESS HINCHINGBROOK, BY THOMAS LAWRENCE AND STUDIO. THOMAS LAWRENCE, PUBLIC DOMAIN, VIA WIKIMEDIA COMMONS.

OVERLEAF:
THE THREEE AGES OF NAPOLEON

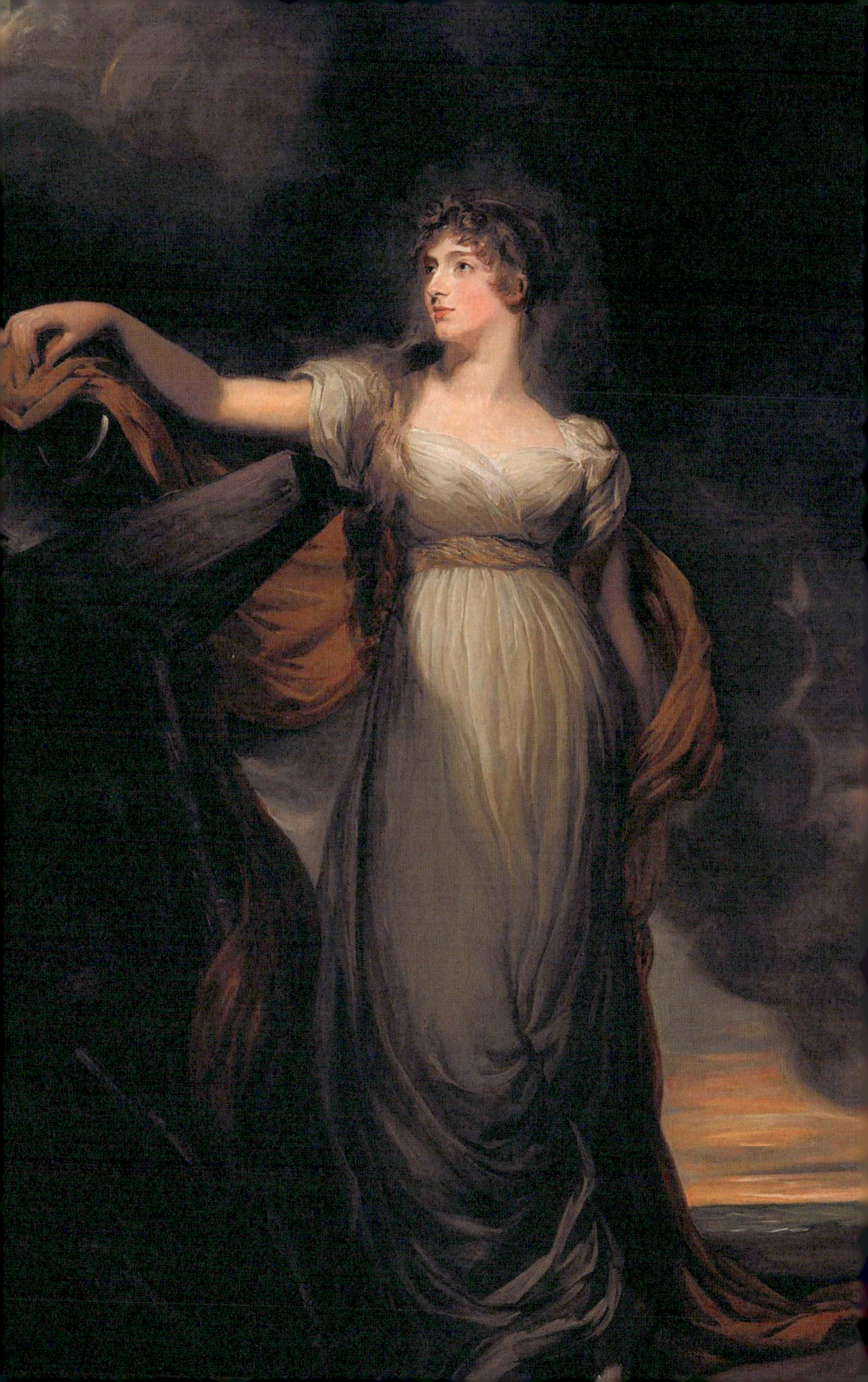

AVANT. PEN[E]

Lith. de V. Ratier

Léclei 1829.

APRÈS.

44

For a cough

Laudanum is tincture of opium, a preparation that contains ten percent powdered opium in an alcohol base. Up until the early 20th century, it was very popular as a cure for coughs and diarrhoea, and was used in many popular remedies. Many authors and artists used laudanum, both Lord Byron and Percy Bysshe Shelley were users. Due to its addictive qualities, it is available now only on prescription.

Take:
½ a pint of best white vinegar
½ a pound of treacle
2 teaspoonfulls of laudanum
Shake them well together, take a dessertspoonful when the cough is troublesome.

OPPOSITE:
THE OPIUM POPPY

For the hooping cough

Whooping cough, or petussis, is a highly infectious bacterial disease, characterised by a distinctive cough sound. It is vaccinated against today, but still kills a large amount of people. The ingredients in this recipe include hartshorn – which was made of shavings taken from deer antlers, dissolved in spirits, and oil of amber, which is made by melting amber.

Rub the back bone every night going to bed with old rum. The palms of the hands, the soles of the feet, and pit of the stomach every night and morning with an equal quantity of spirits of hartshorn and oil of amber mixt together.

Receipt for the bite of a mad dog

Cinnabar is the ore of mercury. It has a bright, rich, brick red colour, and was often used in Chinese lacquerware. It is highly toxic, due to its mercury content, and it's surprising to see it here as its toxicity was known as far back as ancient Rome.

Factitious cinnabar is artificial cinnabar made by subliming a mixture of mercury and sulphur to make a red powder which is used as a pigment.

Musk deer, small creatures hunted for their musk glands, are the source of musk. They live in Russia and the mountains of northeast Asia. Each component of this recipe is dangerous taken orally in its own right, but rabies is a deadly disease, so perhaps they felt it was worth the risk.

Today the treatment for rabies is PEP, Post-exposure prophylaxis where the patient is repeatedly injected with immunoglobulins and rabies vaccine. Without prompt attention, rabies is fatal. In 1885 a vaccine was developed by Louis Pasteur and Émile Roux.

Take 24 grains of native cinnabar, 24 grains of factitious cinnabar and 15 grains of musk let them all be ground into very fine powder and taken in a small teacup of arrack brandy or rum, as soon as possible after the bite and another dose 30 days after and may take another 30 days after that if they please but if the symptoms of madness appear on the person they must take two of the above doses in an hour or an hour and a half at farthest and may take another next morning if there be occasion.

MUSK DEER

For the gravel (or gravit)

I'm not sure what exactly gravel or gravit is, but Hawthorn Berry used to be made into jam, and is a source of vitamin C, vitamin D, and antioxidants. It has been used since the middle ages as a heart tonic, and also to help with circulatory diseases. It was also eaten raw, when in season, and the hawthorn trees in the Irish countryside were stripped bare by children eating the berries as recently as thirty years ago.

ABOVE:
HAWTHORNE

Dry in an oven or otherwise, the red Hawthorn Berry then pound it stone and all into a fine powder, and take on an empty stomach so much of the powder as will be on a sixpenny piece in a small glass of white wine, to be taken every day.
The above is for a grown person.

For an ague

Ague is the old word for Malaria, a disease transmitted through the bite of a mosquito. Nowadays, we tend to think of Malaria as being a tropical disease, but in the 18th and early 19th century it was a common complaint in Europe.

Peruvian Bark is the bark of a variety of trees of the category Cinchona, and is the source of the most effective cure for Malaria, quinine.

Peruvian Bark was also known as Jesuit's bark as it was brought to the attention of the western world by Jesuit priests working in Peru. It would have been dried and ground into a powder for use.

An electuary is a paste – and an emetic is a substance taken to induce vomiting.

Today, malaria is protected against by the taking of anti-malaria tablets.

Six drachms of Peruvian Bark – half a drachm of salt of steel – half a drachm of cloves – made up into an electuary with syrup of cloves – the quantity of a nutmeg to be taken every three hours so that the whole of the above quantity may be taken between the fits. An emetic is recommended before you commence taking the medicine. This dose is to be repeated at the expiration of a fortnight to prevent a return of the complaint.

CINCHONA - SOURCE OF PERUVIAN BARK

Eye water

This recipe for an eyewash uses white copperas, which is zinc sulfate which was used as an astringent. The system of measurement drachm, is a unit of measure in the apothecaries' system, which was calculated in fluid measures. A drachm is 1/8 of a ounce, and is equal to 3 scruples, or 60 grains.

One drachm white copperas, one drachm camphor one drachm Armenian bole mixed in a quart of hot water and just given a boil. When cold 'tis fit for use. If the eye is much inflamed take off the cold when you use it.

Cure for the hooping cough

Salt of Tartar is Potassium carbonate, the primary component of potash. Potash was baked in a kiln to remove impurities and the fire white powder remaining was called pearl ash, or salt of tartar. It has been used as a baking agent.

The unit of measure, nagin (or naggin) is usually 200ml.

Cochineal is a red substance formed from ground up cochineal scale insects, which live on cactus plants in Central and North America. It was used primarily as a dyestuff, and was much prized by the Aztecs and the Maya. It was so valuable for dying fabrics, that it was quoted as a commodity on the London and Amsterdam commodity exchanges. Today, it is often used in the manufacture of cosmetics, including lipstick and rouge, as well as being a natural food colouring used in food.

Dissolve one scruple of salt of tartar in one nagin of water, add to it ten grains of cochineal and sweeten it with lump sugar to make it palatable. Given an infant under two years old the fourth part of a tablespoonful four times a day. To a child from two to four years of age given half a tablespoonful, four times a day. To each patient given a spoonful of barley water after each time. This relieves in twenty four hours and cures effectively in six or seven days. To a person four year old and upwards let an entire tablespoonful be given each time, and a spoonful of barley water be given each time.

INDIAN COLLECTING COCHINEAL WITH A DEER TAIL
JOSÉ ANTONIO DE ALZATE Y RAMÍREZ (1737-1799)., PUBLIC DOMAIN, VIA WIKIMEDIA COMMONS

Mumps

Mumps is a viral disease, and today is immunised against. There is no specific treatment for mumps today, although the application of heat and cool dressing to the swelling in the neck may cause some relief.

Sal ammoniac is ammonium chloride. It was traditionally used to soothe the pain of sore throats, with a paper cone being inserted into the throat of the patient, and then powdered sal ammoniac was blown down the cone. The dust stuck to the painful spot causing instant relief.

½ an ounce of sal ammoniac
A naggin of spirits
A naggin of vinegar
2 naggins of water

This mixture to be warmed and applied upon a soft piece of linen to the glands when swelled by mumps.

Recipe for Rheumatism – Bowes Daly

Denis Bowes Daly was an Irish politician who was elected at the United Kingdom General Election of 1802 to serve as Member of the 2nd United Kingdom Parliament from Ireland. He represented Co. Galway. At the same time, Nathaniel Clements represented Co. Leitrim.

The first three ingredients in this remedy are derived from trees. Rosin is derived from pines and conifers. Frankincense is resin from the Boswellia tree, and has been used for hundreds of years as a cure for arthritis. Stone pitch is from the Stone Pine tree, cultivated for thousands of years for its edible pine nuts.

STONE PINE

1 lb of white rosin
half a lb of frankincense
quarter of a lb of stone pitch
a quarter of a lb of mutton suet rendered.

Dissolve them in an earthern dish and spread it thin and evenly on coarse brown paper, to be applied to the part affected, and left till it falls off. If necessary put on a second.

It should never be used where there is swelling or inflammation.

It is very good for weakness after a strain, and a good warm plaister for a cough either applied on the back or chest.

For an ague
Given and recommended by Miss Graham

Cobwebs are rich in Vitamin K, and were often used to stop bleeding in cuts, when applied externally. In this remedy they are used as a cure for malaria. There are quite a few instances documented from the mid 1700's to the mid 1800's of the efficacy of these pills made of cobweb as a cure for malaria.

Make six pills of cobweb, picked clean, mixed with bread or anything that will combine them. Give one half an hour before you expect the cold fit. Two the next time you expect the fit to come on, and three the third time.

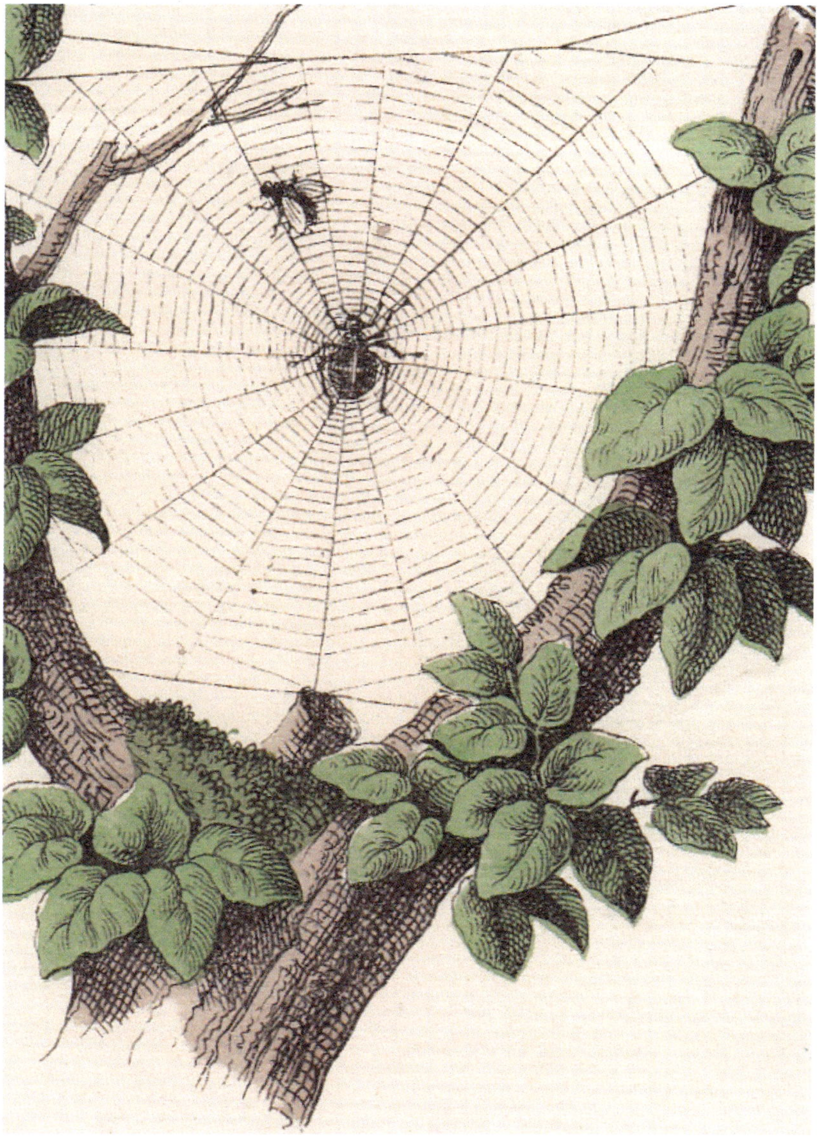

Recipe for a sore throat or thrush
Given by Miss Graham

Woodbine is also known as honeysuckle. Its Latin name is Lonicera periclymenum and it has been used in herbal medicine as an antiseptic and a mouthwash, and is supposedly good for mouth ulcers and gargles.

Sage has always been an important medicinal plant, especially in medications for sore throats and mouth ulcers.

One handful of sage leaves
One handful of woodbine leaves
One handful of southern wood
One handful of sweet briar tops

All well picked and washed. Put them into a pint of honey, add a quarter of a pound of white sugar, let it simmer over a fire for twenty minutes in which time all the juice will be extracted. Squeeze it through a coarse cloth and bottle it for use. Take a teaspoonful as often in the day as the throat feels dry, and continue until it is quite well.

SOUTHERNWOOD

To prevent the spreading of an infectious fever

Saltpetre is potassium nitrate. Today it is often used as an ingredient in toothpaste for sensitive teeth. Rags soaked in salt petre and burned are used to fumigate bee hives, as they make the bees sleepy.

Take an ounce of saltpetre to which add as much hot water as will dissolve it; then draw shreds of writing paper through it, and when dry burn them in the sick room frequently and occasionally in other parts of the house.

ABOVE AND OPPOSITE:
BILLHEADS FROM KILLADOON

Preventive of fever – from the newspapers

Receipt for the prevention of infection from fevers, dysentery etc by Dr. J. C. Smith who got from Parliament 500 l. for the discovery.

6 drachms powdered nitre – 6 drachms oil of vitriol.
Mix these in a teacup by adding to the nitre one drachm at a time of the oil. The cup to be placed during preparation on a hot hearth or plate of heated iron and the mixture to be stirred with a tobacco pipe or a piece of glass. The cup to be changed to different places in the apartment of the sick.

Hoarhound Syrup

Horehound, or marrubium vulgare, is a herbaceous perennial plant which is still used today to make horehound lozenges, which soothe the throat and reduce inflammation of tissues in the throat. It is also used as an ingredient in many cough syrups in Europe.

> **Four quarts of water with one handful of dried hoarhound slowly boiled or simmered down to two quarts, to be these strained and one quarter of a pound of honey then thrown in. To be taken a small wine glass full three times a day.**

HOARHOUND

Receipt to prevent infection from fever

Take rue, sage, mint rosemary and lavender fresh gathered of each a handful cut them small and put them into a stone jar.

Pour upon the herbs a pint of the best white wine vinegar, cover the jar close, and let it stand eight days in the sun or near a fire. Then strain it off and dissolve in it an ounce of camphor.

This liquid sprinkled about the sick chamber or fumigated will revive the patient, and prevent the attendants from receiving infection.

MINT

A truly valuable fumigation powder

The 88th was an Irish Regiment of the British Army, The Connaught Rangers, also called 'The Devil's Own.' They were in Jersey in 1796, and four years later were in India, where they served in Bombay, Ceylon and Madras.

> *Nitre four pounds, sulphur 2 pounds, southern wood and juniper berries of each three pounds, tar and myrrh, a pound and a half.*
> *This was tried at Moscow in 1772, and ten malifactors under sentence of death were fumigated well with this in the Lazarette, and were confined for three weeks in this abode, saturated with infection and made to sleep with persons infected with the plague, and even dead of it and not one was made ill of the disease. The vapour arising from the decomposition of the nitre by the vitriolic acid, is perfectly harmless to be breathed and may be employed in every situation.*

This was used by Mr McGregor, after the plan of Dr Carmichael Smith who relates in 10 weeks at Jersey, he lost in petrified fever 50 men from the 88th regiment, but beginning the fumigation not only the fever was banished from the hospital, but that it change the nature of the existing fever with the malignant symptoms disappeared and to 60 soldiers ill of the fever, not one died.

JAMES CARMICHAEL SMYTH. FELLOW OF THE ROYAL COLLEGE OF PHYSICIANS AND PHYSICIAN EXTRAORDINARY TO HIS MAJESTY.
PUBLIC DOMAIN VIA WIKIMEDIA FROM THE COLLECTION OF THE ROYAL COLLEGE OF PHYSICANS, LONDON.
UNKNOWN ARTIST.

Colonel Wood's recipe

To one ounce of concentrated vitriolic acid, put two ounces of purified nitre. When mixed in a saucer or small plate. Place the same over a lamp to be kept constantly burning in the room of the sick person, renewed when all the fumes have evaporated.

Extract of a letter from Doctor Glass

Does your Lordship know the virtues of the white of an egg well beaten with a little sugar and a quarter of a pint of cold milk and the same quantity of hot water (putting the cold milk first) well mixed and taken as asses milk? I have often found it a wonderful restorative. If Lady Leitrim has never tried it, I should be glad if she might be induced to take it once or twice a day…

Warts

Gum Galbanum is one of the oldest of drugs, derived from a family of umbelliferae plants that grow on the mountain ranges of northern Iran. They are used to derive the 'green' scent in many perfumes, including Chanel No. 19.

Galbanum is an analgesic, and was reputedly good for wounds, cuts and lung complaints. It was used in Egyptian times and was written about by Hippocrates and Pliny the Younger. It also appears in the old testament in the Bible, in Exodus:
Then the Lord said to Moses, "Take for yourself spices, stacte and onycha and galbanum, spices with pure frankincense; there shall be an equal part of each. With it you shall make incense, a perfume, the work of a perfumer, salted, pure and holy."

Diachylon plaster is an adhesive plaster made of litharge and oil, and verdigrease (or acetite of copper) is a kind of green rust formed by applying vinegar to copper.

Warts may be exterminated by ligature. Another method of extirpating them by eviction or plucking them out, but such practice is by no means recommended as the warts speedily return.
A preferable mode of eradicating them, is by the application of escharotics or mild cauteries – for example crude sal ammoniac which must be moistened with water and rubbed on the tumors two or three times every day, or wetting them with the liquid salt of tartar, spirit of hartshorn or tincture of Spanish flies, either of which has been successfully employed for this purpose.
Another mode of exterminating warts, has been recommended by the following plaster. Dissolve one ounce of gum galbanum in vinegar. Evaporate the solution to a proper consistence and add half an ounce of common tar, 2 drams of simple diachylon plaster, 20 grains of verdigrease and an equal portion of sal ammoniac. Let the two last ingredients be finely pulverized, and the whole be duly incorporated. Previous to its application the warts out to be well rubbed with moistened soap, again dried, and the plaster renewed every twelve hours. For obstinate cases however, it be necessary to resort to internal remedies and to change the milk diet of children by allowing them a greater proportion of animal food.

Two notes in different hands end this recipe:
N.B. I had above 50 warts and took them all off with a little aquafortis and water.
 And I had 51 and took them off with the muriat of Iron.

FERULA GUMMOSA. FRANZ EUGEN KÖHLER, KÖHLER'S MEDIZINAL-PFLANZEN, PUBLIC DOMAIN, VIA WIKIMEDIA COMMONS

For burns and scalds and also excellent for inflamed eyes

This recipe is interesting for its use of letharge, today spelt litharge, a natural mineral form of lead oxide. Litharge was used right up until the beginning of the twenty-first century under the alternate name litargirio.

When it is mixed with red lead, the resulting compound is known as litharge of gold. Up until 2003, litargirio, supplied from the Dominican Republic, was commonly available in shops selling herbs and groceries to Hispanic communities in America, who traditionally used it as an antiperspirant and a folk remedy, for the treatment of burns and wound healing.

As both litharge and red lead can cause lead poisoning, litharge of gold is understandably no longer recommended for use on burns and scalds, and you are certainly not advised to bath your eyes with it. The Rhode Island Department of Health has warned against its use since 2003.

Take the common white rose leaves, steep them in best white wine vinegar, press them down with a wooden spoon and as they shrink add more. Once in a day or two for a fortnight or more, strain them off and to a pint of the liquor add a quarter of a pound of Letharge of Gold, put it in a bottle and shake it often for a few days, let it stand on the sediment. A spoonful of it well beaten with a spoonful of sweet oil makes a fine ointment for a scald or burn laid on with a feather. It must be repeated very frequently at first, and will soon relieve the pain and gradually heals the wound.

WHITE ROSE

For an invalid – from Lady Riversdale

The Lady Riversdale mentioned above is likely to be the wife of William Tonson, 2nd Baron Riversdale of Rathcormac in County Cork. They lived in a house called Lisnagar.

Eringo root is the root of eryngium maritimum, the sea holly, which was often candied and pickled at the time.

> ***Half an ounce of candied eringo root, to be put into a pint of new milk and a pint of spring water and to be boiled until only one half remains – it is not to be strained.***
>
> ***The eringo root may be gradually increased to an ounce. The eringo milk is very nutritious, and has been found very efficacious, in cases of extreme weakness and affection of the chest.***

Cure for a cough, cold or asthma given to me by Mrs Lynch at Rosshill November the 29- 1829

Garlic is known to be an effective herbal antibiotic with antiviral properties, and has been used medicinally for thousands of years. The second ingredient in this recipe, liquorice, has anti-inflammatory properties, and is still used by many herbalists as an expectorant. Liquorice root was used by the ancient Romans and Greeks as a cure for coughing and sore throats. Some believed it promoted hair growth and clear vision, and it was even taken as an aphrodisiac. Liquorice has also been found in ancient Egyptian tombs, including that of King Tutankhamun.

The Mrs Lynch who provided this recipe was probably Mrs Lynch of Peterburg, an early eighteenth-century house in the village of Clonbur, which is located between Loch Corrib and Loch Mask in County Galway.

Peterburg was the Lynch family seat in the eighteenth and nineteenth centuries, and the family would have been neighbours of the Berminghams.

Peterburg was acquired by the Land Commission, and divided up, with the lands allocated to local farmers. In 1986 it was sold to the Galway Vocational Education Committee for £1, on the understanding that it would be developed as a leisure amenity for the people of Galway. Today it is an outdoor education centre.

Boil one lb of garlic and four ounces of liquorice root to three quarts of water, reduced to two by boiling. After the garlic is boiled, strain it before you add any of the other ingredients, and lose as little of it as possible.
While the liquid is hot, slice the liquorice ball and pound two ounces of sugar candy. Add these, and boil it slowly until both are dissolved. When almost cold, add a glass of vinegar, or the juice of three lemons, three glasses of spirits and half a pint of good clarified honey. Let it not be bottled until quite cold. Bottle and cork it as close as possible, covering the bottles with leather.
Take a wine glass morning, noon and night while it lasts.

Mrs Ladeveze's cure for the lumbago – deemed infallible

Mrs Ladeveze is probably Dorothea Ladeveze-Adlercron, who lived in both Moyglare in Co. Meath and at Woodville House, Lucan. Gum ammoniac is gum resin from the Dorema Ammoniacum plant, which is a plant from the umbelliferae family of plants, also known as the carrot or parsley family. They are typically aromatic, with hollow stems. Gum galbanum is also derived from umbelliferae plants. Apparently, this gum smells horrible, and I imagine that it would have been particularly unpleasant in use!

__Rub equal quantities of gum ammoniac and of spirit of turpentine, in a mortar, when well incorporated put it into a gallipot. When used it is to be spread on thin leather (glove leather is the best) and applied to the loins, rubbing it with the hand till it sticks close to the skin. As the edges dry, they may be cut away, but the plaster is not to be removed till it fall off, and then a piece of flannel is to be substituted in its place, which also may be cut away by degrees, as cold might bring on a return of pain.__

Pomade Divine
Mrs General Brown

Pomade divine or pommade divine was an ointment or balm used for healing the skin from burns and other skin problems. It was hugely popular in the early 1800s, and can be bought today following a variety of original formulations.
t
The ingredient gum storax is the resin of the Liquidambar orientalis, or oriental sweetgum tree, from Turkey. There are also some of these trees in Rhodes. Its use in perfume adds a deep base note similar to cinnamon and vanilla. It acts to deepen and enhance other scents that it is mixed with.

Florentine orris is the root or the Florentine iris, Iris Florentina, which when dried is very sweetly perfumed with the scent of violets, and is the source of most violet perfumes.

Gum Benjamon or Benjamin, is the gum from trees of the genus, Styrax, which is used in the manufacture of perfume and cosmetics.

Take three pints of rose water, three ounces of gum storax. Of Florentine orris and Cyprus nuts, gum benjamon and cinnamon an ounce and a half.

Nutmegs and cloves, of each, three quarters of an ounce.

These ingredients must be all beaten to a coarse powder and boiled in two pounds and half of beef marrow with the rose water, then strained off and beat till cold. Put it then into small pots, but be sure not to cover them till the pomade is quite cold.

IRIS GERMANICA FLORENTINA.
FRANZ EUGEN KÖHLER, KÖHLER'S
MEDIZINAL-PFLANZEN, PUBLIC DOMAIN, VIA
WIKIMEDIA COMMONS {{PD-US}}

For a pain in the face from Lord Middleton
Given by Mrs General Brown

The Lord Middleton mentioned in this recipe may have been Henry Willoughby, 6th Baron Middleton who died in 1835, or his successor, Digby Willoughby, 7th Baron Middleton. The Willoughby family seat was at Wollaton Hall, in Nottinghamshire.

King's American Dispensatory, 1898, written by Harvey Wickes Felter, M.D., and John Uri Lloyd, Phr. M., Ph. D. defines spirit of soap as a mixture of shavings of castille soap, alcohol and water, melted together.

Hungary water was the first European perfume, supposedly mixed for a Queen of Hungary in the late 14th Century. The oldest surviving recipes for Hungary Water contain a distillation of rosemary mixed with brandy. It remained popular until the 18th century invention of eau de Cologne, and as well as a perfume, was also used as a remedy, for external application and also to drink. Later recipes also included lavender, mint, sage, marjoram, costus, lemon and orange blossom.

Spirit of soap and Hungary water of each an ounce, half an ounce of liquid laudanum to be well mixed together. Rub some of this with your hand on the part affected.

To cure deafness if occasioned by cold Mrs General Brown

Salt petre, or potassium nitrate, was derived from crystallised deposits in cave walls, or guano (bat's droppings). There are many old recipes that use dissolved salt petre as a remedy for earache.

A tablespoonful of unrefined salt petre, dissolved in a quarter of a pint of cold spring water. A teaspoonful to be thrown into the ear affected for six or seven nights at bed time.

Elder ointment
Mrs General Brown

The Elder tree, Sambucus nigra, has been known for centuries for the health giving properties of its berries and flowers. The leaves of the elder tree are effective as an insect repellent, and elderflower cordial and champagne, together with elderberry wine, are still very popular today. Elderflower ointment can still be found for sale today, as a remedy for chapped skin, burns, cuts and bruises.

> *One lb of elderflowers picked from the stalk. One lb of hogs lard, boil it above half an hour and strain it through flannel. It is good for cuts, bruises, strains, chapped hands or lips, or to heal the skin when the bones come through. It is good for man and beast. The hogs lard should be free from salt.*

ELDER

On the early treatment of the cholera
This advice is from Doctor Quinn, who treated the disease in Germany with extraordinary success

Cholera is an infection caused by a bacterium, Vibrio cholerae. Spirits of wine, as mentioned earlier, is brandy, and gum camphor is derived from the camphor tree, and is a powerful natural antibiotic.

The proportion of spirits of camphor which I made use of, is in the proportion of one part of gum camphor to six parts of strong spirits of wine (two drachms of camphor, to an ounce and a half of spirits of wine.)

I must remark that the spirit of camphor is of no use if not employed in the earliest stage of the disease. Those medical men who have had no opportunity of observing its almost miraculous power in arresting this dreadful malady when it is given in time, have been led to speak lightly of it. In their cases the remedy has been applied too late, and I have scarcely ever seen it fail when administered in the beginning of the attack.

In fact it generally happens that the physician does not arrive in time, before he arrives the disease has often got beyond his reach – but the parents and friends of the person may do wonders and leave little for the medical man; if they give the remedy prescribed immediately after the attack.

The way to administer it is this – two drops of the spirit of camphor to be given with a little sugar and water, every five minutes till the symptoms begin to yield, or rather cease augmenting in intensity.

If the vomiting should be so violent as to make it difficult for the stomach to retain the medicine, a small piece of ice about the size of a large nutmeg must be given before and after the camphor.

I again repeat, that no time is to be lost after the disease has declared itself, as its strides are dreadful and a few hours may render the case hopeless. The above prescription and advice was sent to me by Lady Meath.

From Sir William Pym, the head of the medical board in London
Sent to me by Lady Meath

Lady Meath's name before her marriage was Lady Melosina Adelaide Meade, she was the daughter of the 1st Earl of Clanwilliam. She married John Chambré Brabazon, 10th Earl Meath in 1801. Her husband and Nathaniel were Lord Lieutenants of Ireland at around the same time, Nathaniel for Leitrim in 1831, and John for Dublin in 1830. They lived in Kilruddery, an Elizabethan Revival mansion in County Wicklow.

Catechu is prepared from parts of the shrub, Uncaria gambier, which is grown in parts of Asia including Singapore, Malaysia, and Indonesia. Catechu is a powerful astringent, and would have worked to shrink the swollen lining of the intestines. It is still used for the treatment of diarrhoea today.

Sir William Pym was the chairman of the central board of health during the epidemic of cholera which attacked England in 1832.

Diarrhoea or loosenings of the bowels is very often the commencement of cholera, the following draught ought to be taken whenever there is the slightest suspicion of the complaint.
Tincture of Catechu– Zij 2 drachms,
Laudanum – 25 drops
Peppermint water – one ounce
Mix.
The person attacked ought to go to bed immediately and encourage perspiration and send for the medical man. Three or four of the above draughts ought to be kept ready in every family.

UNCARIA GAMBIR.
FRANZ EUGEN KÖHLER, KÖHLER'S
MEDIZINAL-PFLANZEN, PUBLIC DOMAIN, VIA
WIKIMEDIA COMMONS {{PD-US}}

Recipe for Consumption
Given to me by Mr Henry of Lodge Park

Lodge Park is a house near Killadoon, in the neighbouring village of Straffan.

Consumption is the old word for tuberculosis, a disease that was often deadly in the 1800s, with one in four deaths in 1815 attributable to the disease. It is now treated with antibiotics.

Snails were used as a tuberculosis cure all through the 1800s, with many eminent French doctors prescribing them as a remedy.

Ground ivy is Glechoma hederacea, an aromatic herb from the mint family. It is both edible and medicinal, and has always been an important medicinal herb, having both anti-bacterial and anti-viral qualities. Research is ongoing with ground ivy as a remedy for Leukemia, Bronchitis, Hepatitis, many kinds of cancer, and HIV.

Aspic bane cannot at this stage be identified. But plants ending in bane were traditionally poisonous, with the word before them an indication of what they were poisonous to. For example wolfsbane contained a poison that would kill wolves (and werewolves), and other examples would be fleasbane, henbane, leopard's bane, dog's bane, and bug bane. Hence the phrase 'to be a bane of its existence.'

> *Take five quarts of shell snails, one handful of ground ivy, one handful of horehound, one handful of aspic bane leaves and half a pound of liquorice stick.*
> *Put these into ten quarts of water covered closely, and boil them until reduced to five quarts. Then strain the mixture, adding half a pound of sugar candy and half a pound of soft sugar. Put it over a slow fire and skim it till quite clear then take it up and let it remain until quite cold when it may be bottled and kept corked closely.*
> *A small teacup full of the above is to be taken morning and evening.*

To put back a whitlow

A whitlow is an infection of the side of the finger, next to the fingernail.

Potatoe water as hot as can be borne, put the finger into the potatoe water as nearly boiling as you can bear it until the whitlow is dispersed.

For the tooth ache
Lady Elizabeth Clements

The first distillation of wine into brandy was called spirits of wine. Second and subsequent distillations produced rectified spirits of wine. Oil of box was an essential oil obtained from the box plant, often used today in hedging. The essential oil is used today in dentistry, but obtaining it could be difficult as all parts of this plant, Buxus sempervirens, are poisonous.

Two drachms of rectified spirits of wine. One drachm of camphor, Five grains of pure opium. Ten drops oil of box, mix them for use.

Recipe for a sore throat from Mrs Henry, the 2nd of November 1835, as made by her for Lord Massereene

Lady Mary's mother in law, Lady Elizabeth Clements, had been a Skeffington before her marriage, and was the daughter of Clotworthy Skeffington, 1st Earl of Massarene. The Lord Massereene mentioned here, is John Skeffington, 10th Viscount Masserene.

One part hartshorn,
one part camphorated spirits,
two parts oil,
one teaspoonful of Laudanum.
Mix these in a small bottle, and shake it well before using. Rub the throat well with this mixture, and put a piece of new flannel around the throat when rubbed.

Doctor James's recipe for colds sent by Lady Conyngham, the dowager, for Lady Louisa Clements, and from her to me

Lady Conyngham was Elizabeth Conyngham, the mistress of King George IV. She became his lover in 1819, when he was Prince Regent, and remained as his mistress until his death in 1830. HSH Princess Dorothea von Lieven, a Baltic princess who was married to the Russian ambassador, said she had: "not an idea in her head…not a word to say for herself…nothing but a hand to accept pearls and diamonds, and an enormous balcony to wear them on."

> *Take a large teacupful of flaxseed, one ounce of stick liquorice, a ¼ of a lb of sun raisins. Put them into two quarts of soft water, let it simmer on a slow fire until it is reduced to one. When strained, add a quarter of a lb of brown sugar candy pounded, a tablespoonful of old rum, the same quantity of lemon juice. Drink half a pint going to bed, and little when the cough is troublesome.*

What piles of wealth hath she accumulated to her own portion

"Do you think I care for the opinions of any of you"

THE DEEPÔT

Efficacious remedy for cough

Furze, or gorse, is a thorny, evergreen shrub with bright yellow blossoms, that grows wild all over Ireland. The flowers are edible and can be also used in salads.

Gather a large tea cup full of the furze blossoms, which are to be had almost every season of the year. Put them into a tea pot, and pour boiling water on them in the same manner as making tea and let it stand by the fire about fifteen minutes. Pour the water into a cup and sweeten with sugar or honey and add cream.

It may be taken at breakfast as a substitute for tea or may be used before breakfast or on going to bed and will be found a pleasing and effective remedy for a cold almost in every case if timely taken.

The writer of this has frequently experienced its good effects for more than forty years.

Cough lozenges from Lady Elizabeth Clements

Balsam of tolu is the resin of Myroxylon balsamum, a tree that grows in Venezuela, Peru and Colombia. It is still used as an ingredient in cough syrup today.

Gum Arabic is a hard gum derived from the sap of two species of the acacia tree, natives of Africa, and also grown in Asia and Arabia. It is used as a stabiliser in food preparations today, with the E number, E414.

Emeric tartar, which is potassium antimony tartrate, is now acknowledged to be a poisonous ingredient. It was used in old recipes as an expectorant.

2 scruples of purified opium
2 drachms of tincture, or balsam of tolu
2 ounzes and a half of gum Arabic in powder
8 grains of emeric tartar
On going to bed let one of the lozenges dissolve in the mouth, and if the cough is troublesome take another.

A receipt for a cold cream from Lady Floyd

Take a quarter of a pound of white lilly root, half a pound marsh mallow root, wash them very well and cut the roots into thin slices.

Take also, two pounds of quite fresh mutton suet, pick off all the stringy parts. Clean and break the suet into small pieces. The roots and suet must be soaked for 24 hours in a bason of rose water.

After that, the suet must be well worked with the hands in the rose water, then the suet and roots put into an earthen put, and boiled in a bain marais for four hours over a slow fire.

The ingredients must not boil too quick, or burn. Before you put them on the fire, add 4 ounces of spermaceti – when boiled strain the whole into a bason. When nearly cold, add four ounces of oil of almonds and all very well beaten together with a wooden spoon. It will then become white and smooth.

Put it into earthen pots tied close and keep it in a dry cool place. Keeping it becomes hard – in which case work it up again adding a little oil of almonds.

It keeps a long time. The friend whom I had this receipt said, that she knew it to be excellent for the skin.

MARSHMALLOW

FOOD & DRINK

In this section on food and drink, the text of the recipe is faithfully reproduced from the original—spelling and all.

As a result, the measurements are vague, the methods possibly unsanitary when compared to today's standards, and some of these recipes have undoubtedly questionable ingredients.

Enjoy reading them, and be careful if making them!

Receipt for Roasting a Rib of Beef

To bone it, roll it up, flatten it at each end, to look like a filet of veal.

To make a soup of the bones of the Rib of Beef

Of interest in the following recipe, is the use of chyan pepper, which today we call chilli pepper. Chillies were often used in recipes of the period, in fact they were mentioned in William Makepeace Thackeray's book, Vanity Fair, published in 1853.

"Try a chili with it, Miss Sharp," said Joseph, really interested.

"A chili," said Rebecca, gasping. "Oh yes!" She thought a chili was something cool, as its name imported, and was served with some. "How fresh and green they look," she said, and put one into her mouth. It was hotter than the curry; flesh and blood could bear it no longer. She laid down her fork. "Water, for Heaven's sake, water!" she cried.

Put one quart of split peas into four quarts of water, with the above mentioned bones add one head of celery cut small with three turnips, let it boil quietly until it is reduced to two quarts and then work it through a callander with a wooden spoon; mix a little flour and water well together and boil it with the soup, add another head of celery, with chyan pepper and salt to your taste, cut a slice of bread in dice, fry them a light brown and put them into the tureen, after which pour in the soup and serve it up.

Ramoulade Sauce

The following recipe is titled Ramoulade Sauce, but this appears to be an old spelling of what is today called Remoulade Sauce, a popular, mayonnaise based cold sauce, very much like tartar sauce. In modern recipes the herbs parsley and tarragon are often used, and the herb burnet less so. Burnet has a light cucumber flavour, and today Remoulade sometimes includes pickles as an ingredient.

Take some shallots sliced very fine, or some parsley and burnet, minced fine, the yolk of a hard egg, some mustard, pepper, oil, salt and vinegar, mix the whole well together and add a little good cream to it – serve it in a sauce boat, with cold game.

NB: By adding some green tarragon, minced fine and substituting tarragon vinegar for the common vinegar, you make it sauce ramoulade a l'aspic – if you want to make the above sauce in the season when tarragon and burnet cannot be had green, you make the sauce do without them.

Green oil

How exactly this green oil was used is not clear from the following recipe, which details the making of it, but not what to use it for. The ingredient wormwood, is Artemisia absinthum, a dangerous plant from which Absinthe is made. It was used for digestive complaints, and also to rid the body of roundworm and pinworm infestations, but its use has been outlawed as it is classified as a poisonous substance, and absinthe can kill.

Southernwood is a herb of the Artemisia family, which is lemon scented. It is used in Italy as a culinary herb, and in France was used to repel moths and other insects from clothes, its name in French is garderobe. Some alternative names for southernwood are lad's love, and maid's ruin, indicative of the fact that it was supposed to increase young men's virility. It is possible that this oil was to be used as a bath oil, rather than an edible oil, as it must have smelled strongly with southernwood, chamomile, lavender and rose as ingredients.

It is most definitely not recommended for use today, as the wormwood is dangerous.

A quart of the best sallad oil – wormwood, chamomile and southernwood, of each an equal quantity, as much of them as the oil will steep: let the herbs lie a day or two after they are gathered to dry, cut them a little and put them into the oil, with three ounces of fine sugar, pounded fine.

Let it stand a week before you stir it then set it in the sun for fourteen days. At the end of that time, strain the herbs from the oil in a strong cloth very hard.

Then put into the oil lavender tops and the buds of scarlet roses (the white parts taken off) as much as the oil will steep.

When it has stood two days, boil it at least two hours over a very slow fire, take care it does not boil over: then strain it and put to it a quart of the best French brandy, and bottle it for use.

BURNET & OPPOSITE, WORMWOOD

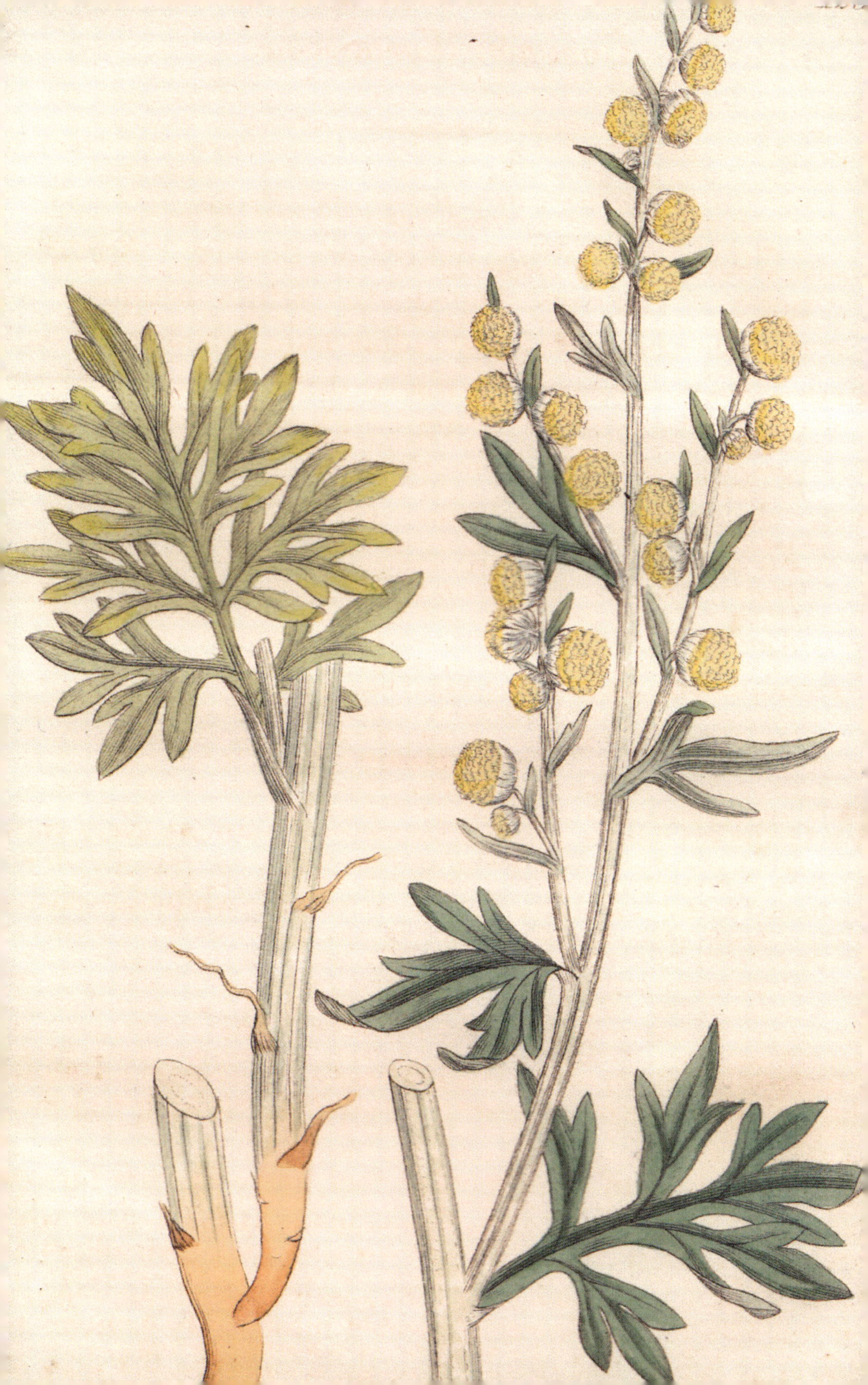

A diet drink of Sir Walter Farquhar's

This recipe uses liquorice root, a common ingredient in the making of drinks today, used for its distinctive, sweet flavour. Docks are wild plants that are well known in Ireland for their properties of taking the pain from nettle stings, which they often grow beside. In fact, even Geoffrey Chaucer in the mid 1380s wrote of docks in Troilus and Criseyde: "Nettle in, dock out. Dock rub, nettle out!" The sharp pointed dock root was useful in the treatment of scurvy, and also believed to be a blood cleanser.

Take, of fresh ground malt-2 ounces
Of sharp pointed dock root, sliced-½ an ounce
Of liquorice root sliced -¼ of an ounce
Boil them in three pints of water over a slow fire to one pint, and strain off the liquor which is to be taken in the course of the day at different times. It should be made fresh every day, and kept in a very cool place.

5 recipes for popular drinks

To make imperial

Take ½ an ounce of cream of tartar to a pint of water, the peel of one lemon, cut very thin, and some sugar.

King's Cup

To one quart of spring water add a quarter of a lb of refined sugar, and the peel of a whole lemon, taken off as thin as possible. Let it stand two or three hours and it will be fit for use.

Diet drink

Take the peel of four lemons and of one Seville orange, and pour a pint of boiling water on them, add half a pound of lump sugar. Take the juice of six lemons and of two Seville oranges in another bason or jug, and pour a quart of boiling milk upon it. Let it stand till the next day, then mix it altogether and strain it through a jelly bag till clear.
NB: If this should not be sweet enough, add more sugar.

Lemonade

To make three pints of lemonade, take the juice of six lemons, add to it the peel of two lemons, cut thin. To which put one quart of boiling water, sweeten it to your taste, and let it stand till quite cold, then pour on it, very quick one pint of skim milk quite boiling and stir it well. Let it stand till quite cold, and strain it through a jelly bag till perfectly clear.

Barley water from Mrs General Brown

When the barley water is made, as soon as it is taken off the fire and whilst nearly boiling put in four of five figs, cut in halves and quartered, a few raisins stoned, a lemon sliced and the peel cut very fine, sweeten it with sugar candy, stir it all well together for some minutes, and put it into a jug with a cover over it to stand till cold. N.B. the above is excellent iced.

Pan Lavato – an Italian side dish

Pan Lavato (washed bread) is a very old savory Tuscan recipe, mentioned by Boccaccio in the 14th century, usually made from bread, tomatoes, onions, cucumbers, basil, oil and vinegar.

Sharpen a handsome slice of white bread that is cut to fill your dish with Seville orange juice sweetened. When it is properly wet, cover it with currant jelly, and thin pieces of blanched almonds all over it. Cut your almonds the long way, but they must be cut thin.

Orange Jelly

Isinglass is a form of collagen made from the dried swim bladders of fish. The fish used was the Sturgeon until 1795, when a cheaper alternative was invented using Cod. In jelly making it has been replaced with gelatine. Isinglass finings are widely used in the 'real ale' brewing process to clarify beer.

Seville oranges are bitter oranges used in making marmalade. Sweet oranges were first cultivated in China and India, and so the china orange mentioned here is probably a sweet one.

> ***Dissolve one ounce of isinglass in a pint of water. Boil three ounces of loaf sugar in half a pint of water and add the peel grated of half a Seville orange. Then add the isinglass jelly and mix it with the sugar over the fire till very hot. Then take it off the fire and stir in the juice of three Seville oranges and when of a proper coolness put it into your mould – if you make your jelly of china orange juice, you put in the peel of two china oranges and the juice of three. Add the juice of half a lemon to it.***

To make a Charlotte

Apple Charlotte is a traditional recipe that is as popular today as it was in Mary's time!

Take two dozen apples and make them into a marmalade. Add some lemon peel, six cloves, a little cinnamon, a few coriander seeds, and about half a pound of sugar. Clarify about half a pound of butter, into which dip slices of the crumb of loaf bread, which is to be put round the inside of a mould of what form you please: then fill it with the marmalade and cover it with slices of the same bread and butter, and put it into an oven of moderate heat for about half an hour.

Artificial yeast

Yeast is used as a leavening agent in baking. It converts the sugars in recipes to carbon dioxide which bubble in the mixture causing it to rise. When the bread or cake is cooked, the yeast dies. Yeast made with potatoes is still used today.

Boil potatoes of the mealy sort till they are thoroughly soft; skin and mash them very smooth, and put as much hot water as will make the mash of the consistency of common beer yeast but not thicker – add to every pound of potatoes two ounces of coarse sugar or treacle, and when just warm stir in for every pound of potatoes two spoonfuls of yeast. Keep it warm till it has done fermenting, and in 24 hours it may be used. A pound of potatoes will make near a quart of yeast, and when made will keep three months. Lay your bread eight hours before you bake it.

New College Puddings

In the 1800s, boiled suet puddings were very popular. This recipe is similar to Spotted Dick, a pudding cooked in a pudding basin. The New College pudding was a variation where small spoonfuls of the mixture were instead fried and then dusted with sugar.

This recipe for New College Puddings, is from New College in Oxford, and is still used today, although the beef dripping is no longer used for frying and butter is used instead. Also, in the modern recipe, they are served with sugar only, the vinegar omitted.

Take half a pound of beef suet, chopped very fine, a quarter of a lb of currants and a quarter of a lb of biscuit pounded, and a penny loaf, grated. 2 ounces of candied orange minced small, the yolks and whites of five eggs, all well mixed together. Add nutmeg and sugar to your taste, then get some butter or beef drippings in a stew pan, and when it is melted, make your mixture in small puddings and fry them. Serve them up with melted butter, sugar and vinegar.

Burnt cream

This delicious pudding is known in French as Crème Brûlée. The earliest known mention of this recipe was in François Massialot's 1691 cookbook, *Nouveau cuisinier royal et bourgeois*. There is no mention of the sprinkling of sugar prior to toasting in this recipe.

In the 18th century, a salamander was a tool for toasting the top of a dish. It consisted of a thick circular plate of iron attached to the end of a long handle held or propped over the dish to be toasted. It was named after the amphibian salamander, which in mythology was supposed to be a creature that could not be harmed by fire.

> *Take a quart of cream, 8 yolks of eggs, some fine sugar, the peel of two lemons. Mix it altogether in a stewpan, then put it on the fire, stirring it till it is smooth and mixed. Then put it into any dish you choose. When it is half cold you must hold a hot salamander to brown the top of it. Garnish it with lemon peel and candied citron.*

Gloucester Jelly

Of particular interest in this recipe is eringo root, which is the root of the sea holly, Eryngium maritimum. This root was widely eaten in candied or pickled form in England, and in other European countries, in the 17th and 18th centuries.

Eringo had a reputation as an aphrodisiac, leading to candied eringos sometimes being called 'kissing comfits.' Shakespeare mentions eringo in The Merry Wives of Windsor, where his character Sir John Falstaff wishes the sky 'hail kissing-comfits and snow eryngoes."

Colchester in England was famed for its Candied Eringo until it went out of fashion in the 1860s.

Hugh Walpole wrote in 'The Bright Pavilions' which he described as an Elizabethan Romance, in 1940:
"Eringo, Eringo, the candied root of sea-holly, whose sharp tang, soaked in sugar with a flavour of burning, he had enjoyed on summer nights at home, lying under the oak tree with a girl, stuffing her mouth with it and then tasting the crisp sugar on her lips."

One ounce of patent sago
One once of pearl barley
One ounce of isinglass
One ounce of candied eringo root.
Boil these ingredients in two quarts of water till reduced to one, a tablespoonful of the jelly in two of warm milk or white wine twice a day. You may add an ounce of rice to the other ingredients and season it with wine, milk or lemon juice with sugar according to taste. When boiled it should be strained through a coarse sieve.

Receipt to make a floating island

Take eight or ten apples peel them and take the pulp off from the core, and put half a pound of them with half a pound of sugar pounded and sifted very fine and the white of four eggs into a pancrock and whip them very well till it comes to a snow whiteness you must have a dish with thick cream at the bottom of it, and dish the whip with a spoon on it.

ERINGO

Receipt for Rice – from Castletown

Castletown is in the same town in County Kildare as Killadoon, at the other end of the main street.

It is Ireland's earliest and largest Palladian house, with a frontage of 380 feet by 84 feet in depth, with two wings and ionic colonnades at the front. It was built between 1722 and 1729 for William Conolly, Speaker of the Irish House of Commons.

J.P. Neale's book, Views of the seats of Noblemen and Gentlemen, printed in 1829, says of Castletown:
In a volume of Excursions in Ireland, printed about sixty years ago, the writer, in speaking of Castletown, the seat of Mr Conolly, the greatest commoner in the kingdom, describes the interior of consisting of a magnificent hall and staircase with massive brass balustrades; a gallery, 86 feet long; three handsome drawing rooms…

½ lb of rice to be well washed and picked, then to be boiled in water when it comes to a boil the water is all to be poured off and as much fresh water put to it.

Boil it again and when it becomes pretty soft pour it on the back of a hair sieve where it should remain until every drop of water has drained off then put it into a stew pan and cover it with milk.

Give it a boil and when it has soaked up all the milk put it on a dish.

Whip up two whites of eggs with some powder sugar, and put it over the top of the rice. You may then put more or less sugar over than as you like it sweet.

Put it in an oven before the fire until it browns.

CASTLETOWN.
KILDARE.

CARTON HOUSE.
KILDARE.
IRELAND.

Paste cakes – Carton

Carton is in Maynooth, a town about four miles away from Killadoon. Carton House was one of Ireland's greatest stately homes, and in the 1750's was the home of Emily, Duchess of Leinster and her family. Emily was another of the famous Lennox sisters-daughters of the Duke of Richmond like her sister in Castletown, Lady Louisa. One of Emily's 23 children was Lord Edward Fitzgerald, leader of the 1798 rebellion. The recipes given in this book by the Duke and Duchess of Leinster, or from Carton, would have been from Augustus Frederick Fitzgerald, the 3rd Duke of Leinster, who married Lady Charlotte Augusta Stanhope, daughter of Charles Stanhope, the third earl of Harrington.

To 1 lb of flour, ¼ lb of butter, a very little salt the yolk of an egg. The butter to be rubbed in the flour to be wetted with water. Cut them what size and shape you please, with a jagging iron. The run should be rather quick, then cakes should be brushed over with the yolk of an egg and milk when put into the oven.

OPPOSITE:
CASTLETOWN (ABOVE) & CARTON (BELOW)

To make cream cheese of that kind of cheese usually called napkin cheese Receipt given by the Duke of Leinster

1 pint of double cream
1 teaspoonful of rennet
Let it stand for three hours then lay it on a fine napkin the size you mean it to be. Lay four or five doubles of linen to dry up the moisture. Put it on a tin laid upon ice.

To make ginger bread.

Gingerbread has been made and enjoyed for centuries.

A pound and a half of flour, takes one pound of treacle, almost as much sugar, and an ounce of beaten ginger. Two ounces of caraway seeds, four ounces of citron, a lemon peel candied, the yolks of four eggs.
Cut your sweetmeats, mix all, and bake it in cakes on tin plates.

A Soufflé

Two spoonfulls of arrow root mixed with one pint of new milk and a quantity of a pint of cream, one ounce of butter, and a little lemon peel. Stir it over a stove till it is thick. When it is a little cold, beat up the yolks of six eggs – the whites must be whipped up and put in just before you put it into the oven. Sweeten it to your taste – a quarter of an hour will bake it. It needs be served up immediately as it is taken out of the oven, otherwise it will fall. It is to be served up in a paper.

Lady Cloncurry's Receipt for making saffron cakes

Until the second half of the nineteenth century, sugar was sold to households in the form of loaf sugar, which were formed in large conical loaves.

Saffron is the world's most expensive spice, derived from the stigmas of the saffron crocus (crocus sativus). It has been used for over three and a half thousand years.

Barm is the foam formed on the top of fermented beer or wine which acted as a raising agent in the production of bread and cakes. Today, we use yeast. Elsewhere in the book there is a recipe for artificial yeast.

> *Two pounds of flour, 2 ounces of butter and two ounces of sugar – rubbed well together. A dessert spoonful of saffron well dried and made fine, boiled in about half a pint of milk. Put a teacupfull of good barm to your flour. In a basin, mix all well together and sit it before the fire until it rises. Mould it up, and make it into small cakes, placed on a tin sheet, let them rise and bake them in a moderate oven.*

SAFFRON

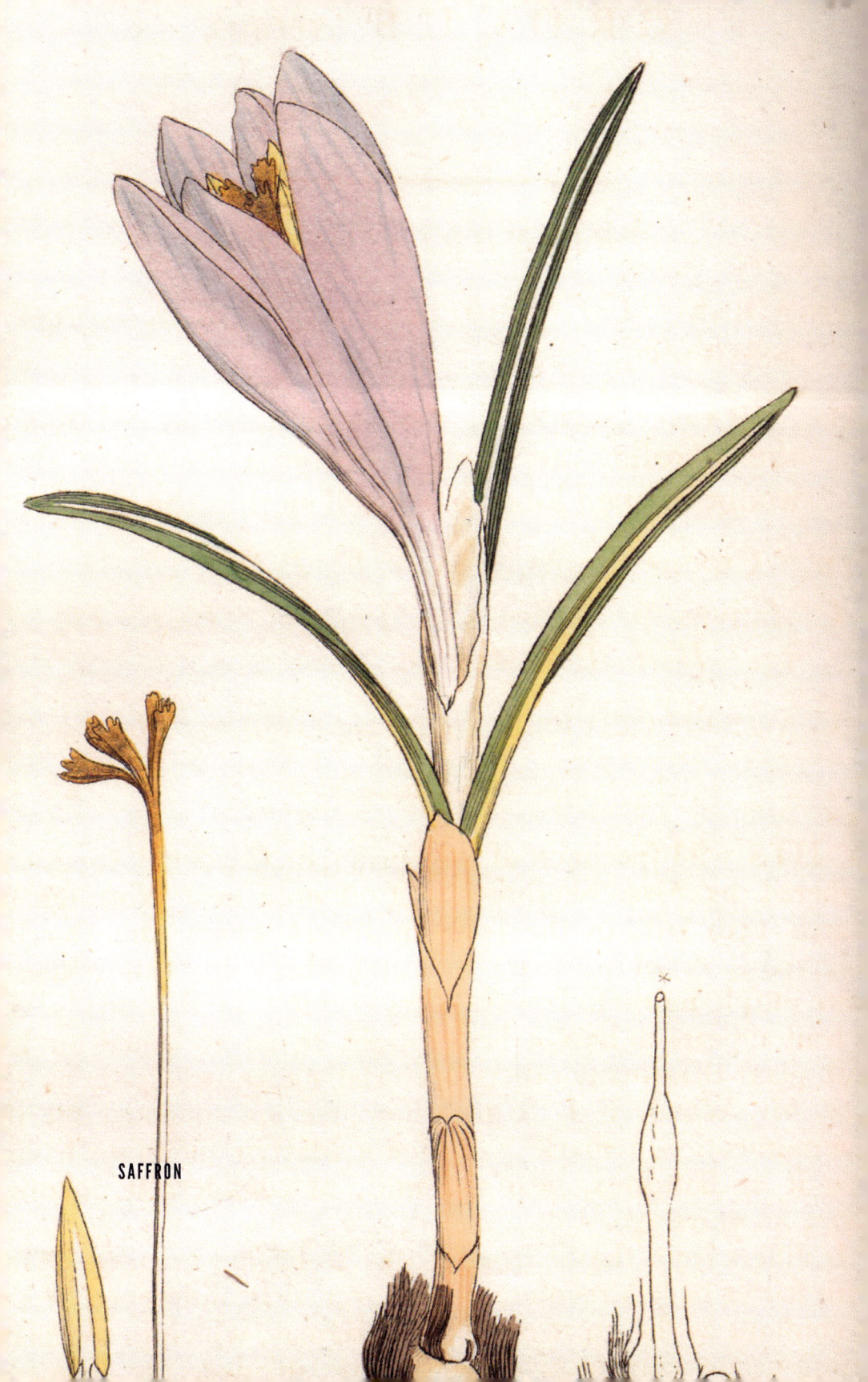

In 1807, Lord Cloncurry's first wife, Georgiana, was involved in a scandal that rocked the establishment when it was revealed that she had had an affair with her husband's old school friend, John Bennett Piers. Lord Cloncurry mounted a 'criminal conversation' trial, in which it was established that Piers had seduced Lady Cloncurry as part of a bet, and a sum of money would be deposited in his account if he were successful. The unfaithful couple had been observed by the Italian muralpainter, Gaspar Gabrielli, who was at the time working in the same room up a ladder. Lord Cloncurry was awarded £20,000 in damages, and was divorced from Lady Cloncurry by an act of Parliament on 26 June 1811. Four days later, he married Emily Douglas, and she became the new Lady Cloncurry.

14 gallons of water – 14 lbs of white sugar, 6 ounces of whole ginger well bruised boiled an hour with the peel of sixteen lemons then add the whites of eight eggs well beaten and take off the scum as it rises. When boiled, strain it into a tub. Let it stand till the next day, then add the juice of sixteen lemons well strained. Put it into a cask with a tablespoonful of ale yeast at the top. Stop the cask close, in a fortnight it may be bottled, and in another fortnight it will be fit to drink.

Lyons is just across the river, visible from Killadoon's drawing room.

ABOVE:
LYONS

To make toasting cakes

Take three quarts of flour, half a pound of sugar, mixed with the flour, a good handful of caraway seeds, about three ounces melted in a pint and a quarter of light milk.
Three eggs well beat up, and half a pint of best fresh bleached barm.
Throw all into the flour, mix it half up, and leave it for half an hour to rise then make it into dough, form the cakes and put them into the oven.
– N.B. Much depends on the inclination of the maker to do them well. The lighter the batter the better for the toasting cakes.

CARAWAY

Buns for breakfast – Mrs Hamilton

Mrs Hamilton was one of the Hamilton's of Hamwood, a Palladian villa built around 1764 in County Meath. The households were always friends.

> *Take two pounds of flour, one pint of milk, four ounces of butter. Put the milk and butter into a saucepan. Keep it over the fire till tolerably hot, take two spoonfulls of yeast and set your spunge.*
>
> *When you see it rise have ready half a pound of soft sugar, and work it into it. Be sure that you do not make your dough stiff.*
>
> *Mould your cakes up into the shape of very small buns, and put them on tins to rise before the fire for a short time.*
>
> *You may add caraway seeds if you choose, they take two hours to bake.*

Lady Rossmore Receipt for drying Irish plums

Lady Rossmore was Augusta, daughter of Francis, Lord Elcho, and was the second wife of William Warner Westenra, 2nd Earl of Rossmore. They lived in Rossmore Park, which was a castle in Monaghan, which has since been demolished.

Stone the plums and have a light sirrup made. Scald them in it, don't let them boil. Repeat this three of four days and as the sirrup gets then add more sugar until you get all the sour out of the plumbs then make a fine rich sirrup and give them a boil in it, and let them remain nine or ten days in this sirrup then take them out one by one and lay them in a sieve to dry. The common horse plum or any large plum will do.

Damson Cakes

Damsons are small plums, usually a dark red colour. They were introduced into England by the Romans, and their stones have been found in digs of Roman encampments throughout Britain.

Put the damsons in a jar in the oven. When they are quite tender rub them thro a sieve. To 9lb and ½ of the pulps, add the white of an egg and 1lb of white sugar sifted then beat them in a large bowl for three hours till quite a thick substance and drop them on paper, peel them in a stove to dry. Care should be taken not to dry them too much. They should be a very bright shade of pink.
N.B. It should be in the above a pound and a half of sugar to one pound of pulp.

Cow Heel Soup

Make a strong clear gravy or five or six lb of fresh lean beef, and boil 2 cow heels in a good deal of water till they are very tender then cut them in small pieces and put them in your soup. Season with pepper and salt, add about a spoonful or two of good white wine according to the quantity of soup but not enough to give it a decided taste of wine. Serve it very hot.

To make a barmbrack

The barmbrack is a traditional Irish yeasted bread, usually with raisins and sultanas in it. This one is interesting, because it has caraway seeds, and no fruit! Barmbrack is often served toasted with butter.

1 lb and ¾ of flour, ¼ of a lb of butter
¼ of a pint of yeast
2 ounces of caraway seeds
½ a pound of sugar
And a pint of milk.
Mix them altogether, and bake it.
The above is the original receipt but as there is often a difficulty about yeast, Dobson often gets the dough ready made from the baker, adding the butter, sugar and caraway seeds. A quarter of dough is the quantity she gets. The great point to be observed, is to lay the dough before the fire, for several hours, till it rises very high and then bake it.
If the dough wants moistening, she adds a small quantity of milk.

A sponge cake
Receipt from Mrs Fisher – Cheltenham

I don't know who this Mrs Fisher of Cheltenham was. Of interest in her recipe is the fact that the weight of the sugar should be 'the weight of 12 eggs' and the weight of the flour should be 'the weight of seven eggs.'

> *Take twelve very fresh eggs. The weight of 12 eggs in loaf sugar sifted, and the weight of seven eggs in fine flour sifted. Beat the eggs about ten minutes. Drop the flour and sugar in by degrees while beating it. Add the rind of a lemon cut as fine as possible and about two tablespoonfuls of brandy.*
>
> *Bake in a moderate oven about an hour and quarter add a little orange flower water if approved.*
>
> *This quantity will make three moderate sized cakes.*
>
> *N.B. four whites not to be put into the cake.*

Dieppe –Navets glacés à la Chartres (Glazed Turnips, à la Chartres)

The archive of Clements papers has letters from Mary to Nathaniel written from Dieppe, in France in 1828. Dieppe became a popular holiday destination to the French royal family - in 1826 the Duchess of Berry, daughter-in-law of King Charles X of France, brought a large party to Dieppe for 'sea bathing'. A 1836 book called Wallis's Royal Edition, Brighton As It Is, 1836, described a holiday at Dieppe thus:

The following summary account of Dieppe may not be uninteresting to the reader, particularly as the general manners and customs of the place present a striking contrast to those of their English neighbours. The appearance of Dieppe from the sea is very striking not so much from the size of the place, as from the contrast of the surrounding scenery. The cliffs on either side of the town, though not high, are steep and rugged, and the ancient castle, which is built on an acclivity East of the town, adds to the wildness of the appearance.
Immediately facing the shore is an elegant building called the Caroline Baths, which was finished in the beginning of the year 1828. The bathing machines, which are not on wheels, are stationed before the building in two divisions, that on the East being allotted to the ladies and that on the West to the gentlemen. The former, when attired in their bathing gowns, are

curried into the sea by men appointed for that purpose, and generally remain there a considerable time, continually jumping up and sinking down with each wave in the most original manner! In the evening the gardens belonging to the baths, and the building itself, form the fashionable promenade of the town.

> **Take 15 or 18 turnips. Peel them and give them the shape of a pear or an olive. Mix a quarter of a pound of butter with two ounces of sugar, cook them till they assume the colour of gold. Then add a dessert spoonful of flour and then a tablespoon of gravy. Let it be reduced to a jelly or thick sauce, and serve them up very hot.**

Fig. 424.

THE SINGLING OF TURNIPS.

INSIDE OUR BATHING-MACHINE.
Owing to the Holes in the Roof, we take some Time to Dress on a Wet Morning.

RUSBOROUGH.

Drawn by J.P. Neale.   Engraved by T. Barber.

Sallelons
Sent by Mr Leeson, January 26th 1832

Joseph Leeson the 4th Earl of Milltown, lived at Russborough, Co. Wicklow.

6 lb fine flour sifted, barm (one third water)
When risen add one pint of milk, 6 whole eggs, well beaten up, put in the last thing. This must be baked in a plumb cake hoop in a moderate oven. The above quantity will make a large Sallilon.
N.B. Should the barm be had from the brewery, no water will be required. The barm alluded to above is composition.

OPPOSITE:
THE BATHING MACHINE (ABOVE)
RUSSBOROUGH (BELOW)

Queen Charlotte's recipe for orange juice Given by Mrs General Brown

Queen Charlotte was the wife of George III, and mother to their fifteen children. She died in 1818.

One pint of Seville orange juice to a lb and a half of lump sugar. Stir it well until the sugar is dissolved. Skim it, and after standing ten days, bottle it and will keep well for years.

OPPOSITE:
QUEEN CHARLOTTE; PRINCESS SOPHIA CHARLOTTE OF MECKLENBURG-STRELITZ, 1744 - 1818.
QUEEN OF GEORGE III NATIONAL GALLERIES OF SCOTLAND,
PUBLIC DOMAIN, VIA WIKIMEDIA COMMONS

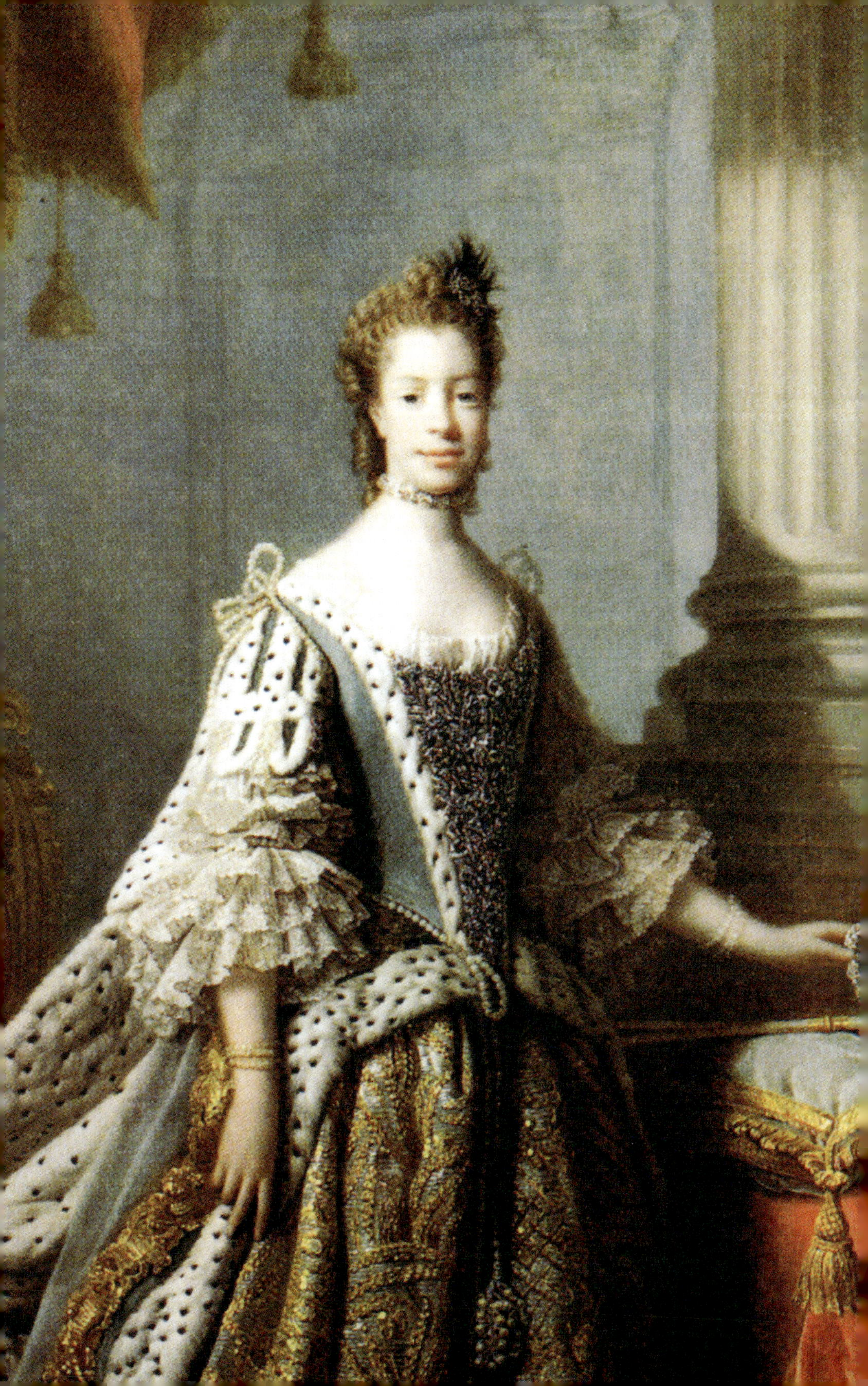

Bread sauce – the ladies in Wales

I believe the 'ladies in Wales' to be the famous 'Ladies of Llangollen', Eleanor Butler and Sarah Ponsonby, who lived within two miles of each other growing up in Ireland, and were devoted to each other. In 1778, keen to escape the prospect of marriage, they ran away together. Despite their families attempts to bringg them home, they set up home together in 1780 in Plas Newydd, near the village of Llangollen. In the years that followed, their home became a haven for many famous people, such as Wordsworth, Shelley and Byron. Queen Charlotte asked to see their cottage, and persuaded the King to give them a pension. The couple lived together for the rest of their lives, and their cottage is now a museum. This picture of 'ladies' has always been at Killadoon.

Take a quantity of the crumb of white bread sufficiently old for the purpose. Grate it pretty fine, put it in a saucepan with some rich and sweet cream, one shallot, a few grains of white pepper and salt it to your taste.
Let it boil gradually over a slow fire (or more to be desired a hot hearth) stirring it occasionally and always one way, to prevent it from forming

lumps, till it is perfectly smooth and fit for serving to table.

It is to be observed that not an atom of butter not a drop of gravy is to be admitted into this composition.

Harrington House Sallad of 1829 Given by Lady Caroline Stanhope at Killadoon 1832

In winter salad, endive, Celery and beetroot in summer (excellent Covent Garden) white goss lettuce cut extravagantly so as to leave none of the green leaves and only prepared when dinner is called for.

For the sauce of both the above salads. One hard boiled egg beat up. The yolk of one unboiled. Four tablespoonfuls of oil, half a spoonful of common vinegar, one of tarragon vinegar, a little salt. (In winter mustard also.) Chervil, burnet and tarragon, chopped up very fine and added to it.

When it comes from the market, the lettuce ought in summer to be kept in a tub of cold water in the coolest place until wanted to be cut up just before dinner, when it ought to be either beat against a dry cloth to dry it, or still better put into an open basket of this shape (sold for the purpose) and moved about quickly from right to left, until the water is thoroughly drained from it, to prevent its losing its crispness.

ABOVE:
DETAIL SKETCH FROM THE BOOK OF RECEIPTS

Crumpets
Receipt given by Lady Caroline Stanhope Killadoon 1832

Lady Caroline Stanhope was the daughter of Lord Harrington, and the older sister of Lady Charlotte Stanhope, 3rd Duchess of Leinster, who lived at Carton in nearby Maynooth. At the time that she provided this recipe, she was unmarried. She became the second wife of Edward Ayshford Sanford in 1841.

Talavera wheat was a variety of wheat described by James Hard, miller of Victoria Mills, Dartford – who was the miller to King George IV, as:

"this kind is far superior to any description of wheat, either foreign or English; and the great advantage it possesses consists in its strength, colour, and sweetness. The reason of there being so small a quantity at market, arises from the fact of its being so unprofitable to the farmer, scarcely producing one crop in three, which I greatly regret, as it is the most valuable grain we have; and, technically speaking, if the flour is properly manufactured, 8 oz. will absorb as much liquor as 11 oz. of that used by the baker."

A batter made with milk warm from the cow and a little yeast.

An iron plate, or griddle, being placed over the fire must be heated through for ten minutes then rubbed over with a little butter and the yolk of two eggs occasionally. To one lb of the best (Talavera) wheaten flour add three tablespoonfuls of yeast after being suffered to rise in the hearth a portion of this liquid paste or batter poured by tablespoonfuls on the heated plate (on the fire ready to receive it) and turned over carefully when it begins to look brown with a knife.

To make Iceland Moss

Iceland moss is a type of lichen (cetraria islandica). English Botany, states: *This Lichen abounds with nutritious mucilage, and is become a fashionable medicine in coughs and consumptions. It is previously infused in water to extract its purgative bitter quality.*

The contributor of this recipe is Mrs Sneyd, probably wife of Nathaniel Sneyd, who was Member of Parliament for Carrick at the same time as Lady Mary's husband, Nathaniel, in the late 1790s.

> *The Iceland moss, to be stepped in cold water about three hours. The water to be thrown off and fresh water put on, and then boiled slowly between three and four hours till it is in a jelly. It is to be strained, and to be seasoned according to orders, like sago – with sugar, milk and wine and lemon juice. It has a less bitter taste when eaten cold. To handfuls of Iceland moss to a quart of water is about the proportion. It must be boiled very slowly simmered on a hot hearth.*
> *From Mrs Sneyd.*

ICELAND MOSS

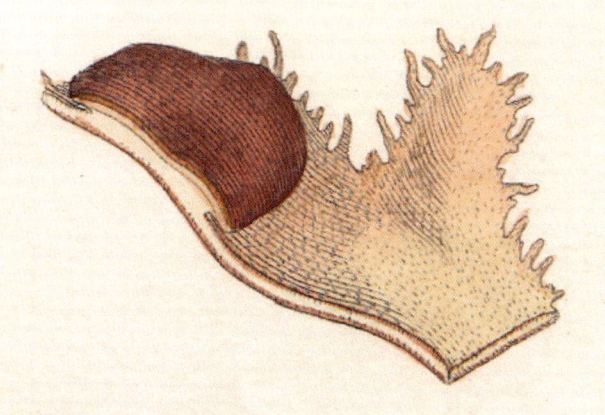

Boiled Sallad from Long Ditton
24th of February 1833

After the death of the first Earl of Leitrim (Nathaniel's father), his widow, Lady Elizabeth and two of her daughters moved to Long Ditton in England. This is their recipe.

Stew the sellary and onions very gently. Boil the beetroot in the ordinary way of boiling it. Mix the egg and mustard well together, then add the oil, and mix it well before you add the vinegar, then a little cream.

Pain à la Duchesse
Translated from French by
Lady Elizabeth Clements

Before 1850, éclairs were known as pain à la Duchesse. These éclairs do not appear to be filled or covered in chocolate, as we are more used to seeing them today but instead are just choux pastry buns.

Put three half pints of water in a very clean stew pan, two ounces of fresh butter, two ounces of sugar the peel of one lemon grated. Put your mixture on the stew hole, observe that the fine must be very clear, stew it till reduced to half, add to it three handfuls of fine flour. Stir all together quickly with a wooden spoon, on a moderate fire, add five ounces of fresh butter by degrees, a little bit at a time. After you have taken it from the fire, you must add five or six eggs one by one, observe to work your mixture well while putting in the eggs. Take then your tin sheets and with two table spoons place them on them about the size of a walnut and you will gaze the outside with an egg. You will bake them in a moderate oven they should look of a bright colour.

A SILHOUETTE OF LADY ELIZABETH CLEMENTS

An Indian dish
From Mrs Hamilton of Hamwood

Wash in several waters, half a pound of rice, then put it into a saucepan with two quarts of water. Do not suffer it to boil until it has been on the fire for near half an hour. You may afterwards let it boil quick till you see the grain swell. You must then strain the water off, and leave it to drain.

Cut five chickens into quarters and take off their skins. Season them with pepper and salt then butter the bottom of a dish and lay them in it, and put over them two onzes of cold butter, a little mace, a few cloves and two or three bits of cinnamon.

Pour into the dish one pint of the water in which the rice was boiled, and cover the whole with a few hard boiled yolks of eggs and the rice, heaping it up like a Pyramid.

Make a paste of flour and water, roll it out very thin, and cover the dish with it making a little hole in the top. Let it bake in a good hot oven for two hours. When you take it out of the oven take off the paste and pour into the hole at the top a pint of good gravy.

N.B. The dish may be lined and edged with pye paste, and the yolks of eggs may be left out.

To make barm

Boil one ounce of hops in one gallon of water for fifteen minutes and strain it. To the strained liquor add four pounds of bruised potatoes, mix them well, and strain them again. Then add, when nearly cool, six tablespoonfuls of flour and the same quantity of brown sugar, keep it in a warm place to ferment, stirring it occasionally. When the fermentation is over, it may be bottled and corked.

A breakfast cup full of the barm is to be mixed with six pounds of flour, and warm water is to be added in sufficient quantity to make dough. It is to be worked well, for half an hour or longer. To be then placed in a warm place till morning, when the dough is again to be well worked with the hand and then formed into loaves and put into the over.

The above receipt Mrs Ponsonby got from an apothecary at Derry, and finds it answer extremely well.

A receipt for dressing seppes
From Mr Barton of Straffan

Straffan is a village a few miles away from Killadoon. Mr Hugh Barton built Straffan House in 1832. He was the grandson of Thomas Barton, originally from Buttevant, Co. Cork, who moved to Bordeaux and set up a wine firm in 1725. By 1747, Thomas Barton was considered Bordeaux's number one shipper, earning him the nickname, 'French Tom.' In 1794 during the Reign of Terror in the French Revolution, foreigners were unable to own lands in France, and Hugh Barton was forced to flee Bordeaux. He left his wine firm in the capable hands of a French trader, Daniel Guestier. Later, in 1802, Hugh and Daniel formed a business, Barton & Guestier, which today is the oldest wine merchant established in Bordeaux.

Straffan House is now a golf club and hotel, renamed The K Club.

The seppes mentioned in this recipe are ceps mushrooms, called cèpes in France. There are two types of cep mushrooms, cèpe de Bordeaux, and Tête de nègre. These wild mushrooms are often dried in a slow oven to rid them of moisture, and then stewed in oil, prior to cooking. In Italy, ceps are called porcini, and another English name for them is 'Penny Bun.'

Take the seppes out of the oil, and wipe them well, then place them in a frying pan with some fresh oil enough to cover them, sprinkle them with salt and mince two shallots or two cloves of garlick, very fine, and put it into the pan with the seppes.

Let them fry for a quarter of an hour, or twenty minutes, when they are dished place the shallots or garlick, which have been fried with them, on the top of each seppe, with a little of the oil.

Arrow root blancmange

Arrowroot is derived from the root of the rainforest plant, Maranta arundinacea. The roots are harvested and processed to produce a fine white powder which is an efficient thickening agent.

Take a pint of milk, boil it with twelve sweet and six bitter almonds, blanched and beaten. Sweeten it with loaf sugar, and strain it. Take a tea cup full of arrow root, break it with a little of the milk as smooth as possible.
Pour the boiling milk upon it, stirring it all the while. Put it back into the pan, let it boil for a few minutes, still stirring it.
Dip the shape into cold water before you put it in, and turn it out when cold.
The above is from Lady Elizabeth Clements.

To make carrageen moss into jelly for invalids from Lady Elizabeth Clements

Carrigeen moss is a type of red algae that grows abundantly around the Atlantic coast of Ireland, Europe and North America. It is the source of carrageenan, which is used as a thickening agent in all sorts of foodstuffs today.

Take one ounce of Carrigeen moss and steep it in cold water, to clean it for a few minutes, then take it out and push it into a stewpan with a pint of cold water and let it come to a boil on a slow fire. It will require to simmer for about half an hour, till it thickens. You may boil a little lemon peel cut very thin in it, and when done, strain it through a sieve and add sugar and lemon juice to your taste.

Orange wafer – Lady Elizabeth Clements

Six very fine Seville oranges, boiled in water till quite tender, then open them to take out all the pulp and seeds.

Chop the rest as fine as possible, then pound it all in a mortar to a paste and rub it afterwards through a coarse sieve.

To the weight of oranges add an equal weight of double refined sugar pounded fine, which must all be again well pounded together then with a bread knife spread it as thin as a wafer on pieces of glass.

Place them in the sun to dry or before the fire, and when a little set, cut the paste in squares with a sharp knife, and turn them every day till quite crisp. The wafers must be kept in tin boxes.

To make Hasty Pudding from Anne Ward August 22ⁿᵈ 1837

Hasty pudding is a very old recipe, with many variations. In the mid 1700's the American Song, Yankee Doodle Dandy, mentions it in one of the verses:

Fath'r and I went down to camp,
Along with Captain Gooding,
And there we saw the men and boys
As thick as hasty pudding.

Put four bay leaves into a quart of new milk and set it over a fire to boil them – then beat up the yolks of two eggs with a little salt. Take two or three spoonfuls of the milk to beat up with the eggs, take out the bay leaves, and stir up the remainder of the milk. Then, with a wooden spoon in one hand, and some flour in the other stir it in (that is the flour) until it is a good thickness but not too thick, then let it boil for about ten minutes keeping at stirring all the time. Then pour it into a deep dish and put pieces of butter in different parts of the dish and sift white sugar over it and serve it up quite hot. Remember before you add the flour to take out the bay leaves.

Goose Grass, or Robin Run the Hedge
A receipt for making it from
Lady Bunbury

Goose grass has a number of other names, including Robin run the hedge and stickywilly. It is said to be high in vitamin C, and a tea of it was made to act as a tonic, laxative and diuretic.

Lady Bunbury is the former Emily Napier (daughter of Lady Sarah Lennox and Colonel the Hon. George Napier, and adopted daughter of Lady Louisa Conolly). She married as his second wife Sir Henry Edward Bunbury, 7th Bt, of Barton, Suffolk. Mary would have known her from Castletown.

> ***Take the young and juicy shoots of the goose grass, and pound them in a mortar fresh every day, and of the juice so expressed and strained, take a half a tea cup full every morning and middle of the day. Some people add a little sugar to take off the mawkish taste.***

Apple Jelly
from Lady Elizabeth Clements

Cut some codlings into pieces.
Boil them in water until the liquor becomes milky. Put it into a jelly bag, and add 3 quarters of a lb of sugar to every pint of juice, boil it altogether about ten minutes, add a small quantity of scotch marmalade, or boil with it a quince or two.
Put a little colour to it when you take it off the fire and put it into pots for use.

COX'S ORANGE PIPPIN.

HOUSEHOLD

In this household section the text of the receipt is faithfully reproduced from the original—spelling and all.

As with all the receipts in this book - many of these would be frowned upon today as causing harm to furniture or household items. And some would be downright dangerous.
Investigate with caution, or just read for an insight into items used in a bygone age!
As usual, they are included for interest's sake, rather than as usable concoctions today.

To clean mahogany

Alkanet root is the root of the plant anchusa tinctoria, which is a plant in the borage family. The roots yield a red dye, often used to colour furniture.
Rose pink appears in many old furniture recipes, but I have been unable to track down exactly what it was!

__Two penny worth of rose pink, ditto of Alkinite root pounded fine, and mixed in a pint of cold drawn linseed oil.__
__If there are any stains in the mahogany, first wash them with soap and water or sour small beer made hot: then rub the mixture on equally all over.__
__If new mahogany, it must remain on two or three days, if not, rub it off immediately, till it is dry, with soft old linen, it ought to be rubbed three or four times every day.__

For making a green paint for rooms

Blue Vitriol is copper sulphate, when heated it turns a sea foam green colour. Spanish white is a pigment made from chalk. Lime wash is made today from lime powder and water, but used to be made by diluting a lime putty.

> *4 lbs of blue vitriol, 1 lb of Spanish white, boil them together three hours in a glazen earthen pan with ten or twelve quarts of water to be kept stirred with a lath. Pour off the sediment and set the sediment in the sun to dry. To be used with size or lime wash.*

General Pitt's receipt for Cordial Balls

General Pitt is most likely General Sir William Augustus Pitt, a long-serving officer of the British Army who was commander of all the British forces in Ireland until 1791. He was in the 1st King's Dragoon Guards, a cavalry regiment, and later in the 3rd Irish Horse Regiment.

Elecampane, or inula helenium, is also known as horse-heal, is a herb that has been used for hundreds of years in veterinary medicine for the treatment of respiratory conditions in horses.

Aniseed or anise, has a distinctive taste and scent, and has been used medicinally as a digestive aid as it is good for abdominal pain, gastric conditions and gas in horses. It is still used today.

Bay berry or Myrica, is an aromatic tree. The berries were believed to be good used in the treatment of bronchitis and inflammation of the gastro-intestinal tract.

Oxymel of Squill, used for coughs, was invented by Pythagoras, who lived in the sixth century before Christ. It was a syrup made of vinegar of squill and purified honey and acted as an expectorant. The Squill or Urginea scilla, is a bulbous perennial plant, and the bulb is used to make oxymel of squill. It is an ingredient in some cough medicines (for humans) today.

Take of:
Gum Ammoniac 2 ounces
Garlick 4 ounces
Elecampane 4 ounces
Sulphur ½ lb
Aniseed ½ lb
Powdered liquorice ½ lb
Bay's berries 2 ounces
Oxymel of Squilles 2 ounces
Oil of Mace 2 drachms

Mix up the above separately powdered, and beat them up with a sufficient quantity of cold drawn linseed oil the size of a pullet's egg, to be given the horse morning and night.

To clean pictures

Take claret and water, made warm, an equal quantity of each, rub this on the picture with a sponge, when this is dry, varnish it over with the froth of an egg whipped up with a little drop of brandy.
The above was given to Lady Massareene as a good receipt but she never tried it – now follows that which she always used.

Make a lather of soap and water, let it be just warm. Dip a sponge in it and wash the picture till no dirt comes from the sponge when you squeeze it. When 'tis quite clean dry it with a soft towel and then rub the picture over with the white of an egg beat up to a froth with a little brandy. Use this with a feather, then wipe off any of the froth which may remain with a soft cloth.
Wash picture frames with small beer made just warm.

To make Pot Pourri

Potpourri is a mixture of leaves, petals and spices, kept to fragrance a room. Today, potpourri is always dried, but in the 1800s and earlier the mixture was sometimes dry, and sometimes a wet concoction. Pourri in French means rotten, and older potpourri would often be mouldy. Potpourri was placed in a china bowl with a pierced lid to allow the fragrance to escape and scent a room.

The borax in this recipe acted as a drying agent. Benzoin resin, also known as styrax resin is a resin obtained from trees in the styrax family. It is a common component in incense, and has a vanilla scent and fixative properties. Orris root is the dried and chopped root of the irish germanica, which has a violet scent. Orris root and Benzoin were often used together in pot pourri recipes as fixatives, to anchor and intensify the scent.

1 ounce of allspice, 1 ounce of cloves, 1 ounce of borax, 1 ounce of benzoin, 1 ounce of nutmeg, 1 ounce of oraice root powder
To be powdered and mixed together with the flowers and salt.

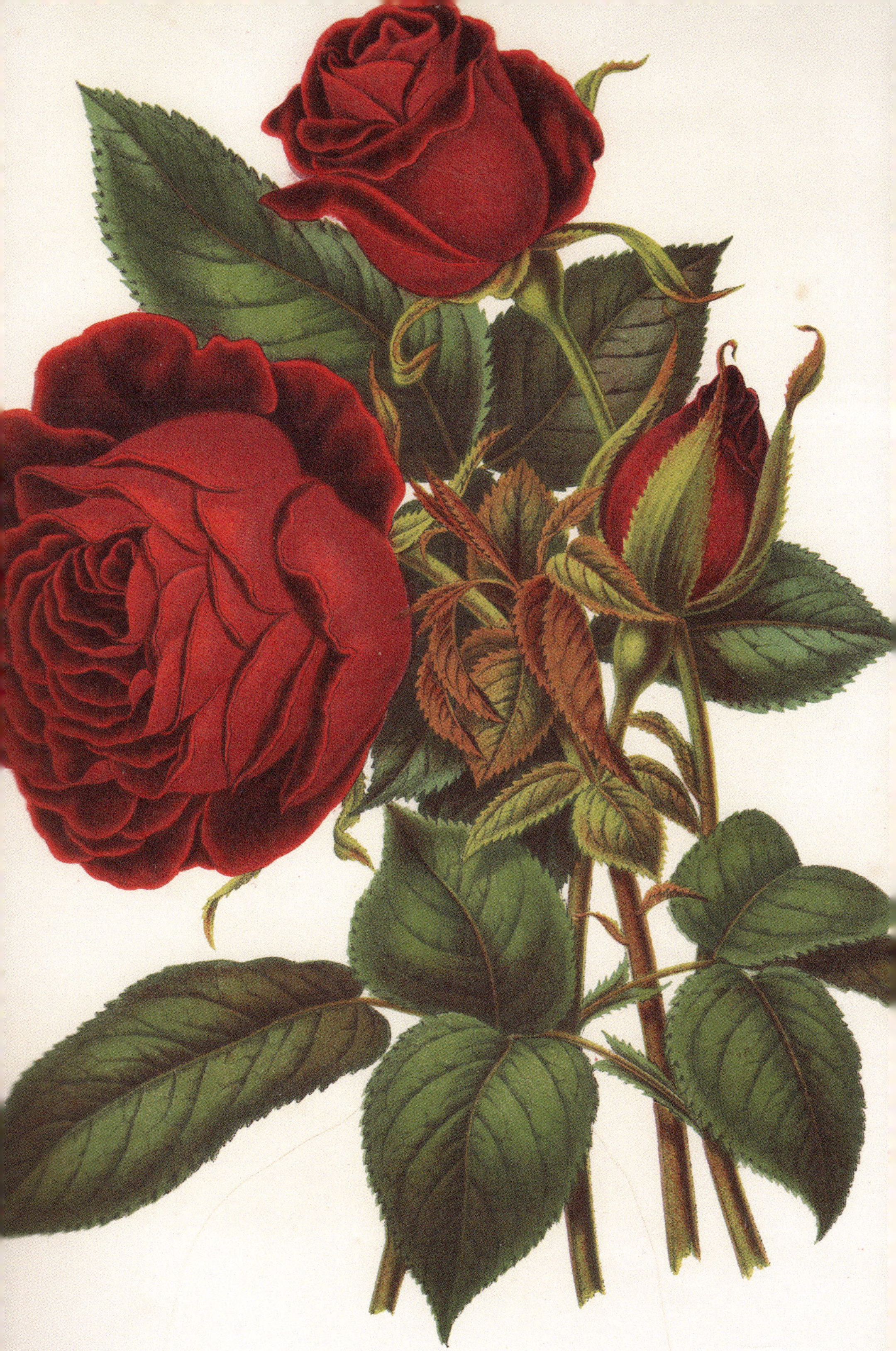

For destroying worms, grubs, etc

Calcium oxide, also known as unslaked lime or quicklime is a chemical compound that has been used for hundreds of years to destroy grubs and worms in the garden, and also used as one of the main components in whitewash (the other being chalk). Also in this recipe is flour of sulphur. Sulphur is one of the oldest fungicides and insecticides, dusting sulphur is used for crop dusting from planes. Tobacco is used in horticulture as a powerful organic insecticide which is deadly to insects.

Six bushels of unslacked lime. Slack it to powder with about two pails of water, and in half an hour after you may add as much more water as will make nearly a butt of liquid. Keep it covered 24 hours, stirring it two or three times. When settled take off the liquid clear and boil in it one pound of the flour of sulphur and half a pound of tobacco the quantity about three gallons. Mix them together again and let it settle. Pour on your land the clear liquid from a garden pot with a rose on it. Three butts with cover an acre.

To render shoes water proof

One pint of drying oil. Two ounces of yellow wax, two ounces of spirit of turpentine, and one ounce of Burgundy Pitch are to be carefully melted together over a slow fire.

Those to whom the smell of pitch and turpentine is unpleasant may add a few drachms of some cheap essential oil as of lavender, thyme and the like with this composition. New shoes or boots are rubbed either in the sun or at some distance from a fire with a spunge or soft brush.

This operation is to be requested as often as they become dry again until they be fully saturated in this matter the leather at length becomes impervious to wet.

The shoes of or boots made of it last much longer than those made of common leather. Acquire such softness and pliability that they never shrivel nor grow hard and inflexible and thus prepared are the most effectual preventative against cold and chilblains.

Browne's Invisible Green

Invisible Green was a dark green paint popular in the Georgian period which made fences appear invisible in the landscape, and so enhanced the view. Mr Humphry Repton, a famous landscape designer of the 1800s, used invisible green on fences and trellises, and Mr William Mason, in his poem The English Garden published in 1783 says:

The means then are briefly these; give to your paling no tawdry glare, but as near as possible the colour of the ground against which it is seen; and thus the eye shall blend them together, and thus the ground in a manner shall absorb the Fence.

The pigment Blue Ochre or vivianite, is a rare mineral of hydrated iron phosphate that is an dark blue colour. Verdigris was used as a drying oil, Blue black was produced by beech charcoal, ground carefully to produce black with a blue hue. the use of white lead often resulted in lead poisoning.

Invisible green still features on many paint manufacturer's paint charts today.

Six pounds of the best Blue Ochre, four pounds of verdigrease, two pounds of Blue Black, two pounds of White Lead.

Directions for preparing and laying Lord Stanhope's Composition as follows

To three measures of ground chalk, sifted very fine and perfectly dry, add one measure of tar – these ingredients when well kneaded together will form a tough dough of a brown colour, which is to be put into an iron pot, and boiled from three to four hours. It will then be reduced to a liquid state of the consistency of boiling pitch – great attention is required when the pot is boiling to keep it stirred and also to know when the composition is sufficiently boiled, which is done as follows: dip an iron rod, piece of slate or tile, into the pot and them put it into a pail of cold water, where let it remain five minutes. If on taking it out, the composition which adheres to the tile or slate is so hard as not to admit of the thumb when pressed against it to make any imperfection but will admit the thumbnail or harder substance to enter it, the composition is then in a proper state for use, and should be laid directly to the thickness of 3/16 of an inch, covering the whole of the slates or tiles in a perfect manner. This covering is called by Lord Stanhope the skimming coat, and will of itself keep out the weather, till it is convenient to lay the finishing coat, which is prepared exactly like the skimming coat – and this requires to be well mixed. The instrument for that purpose should be an iron salver like a plaisterer's, but considerably stronger.

In heating the iron pot, great care should be taken that the fire does not touch it till it has made nearly one revolution round it by a flame, otherwise the tar will burn – there should be one, two, three, or four parts tar, according to the extent of the slab that is to be covered, each part containing about 20 or 25 gallons and three or four small two or three gallon pots will be necessary to carry the composition from the large pots to the slab. The trowels that are used are made up like a plaisterer's trowel and ¾ of an inch thick. Of these there should be half a dozen, and raised hot which will facilitate the laying of the composition and give it a smooth surface.

The pounded chalk should be sifted through a sieve having 24 meshes to an inches square. The sand is of two sized. The smallest must pass through a sieve having sixteen meshes to an inch square, the largest sand through a sieve of ten meshes to an inch, but these are mixed together in equal quantities when wet. The second coat of composition is laid on to the thickness of about half an inch.

It is necessary to leave a spare pot set for the purpose of heating the sand before it is mixed with the other ingredients, which I find makes them incorporate much better.

Directions for making and using the furniture oil called speenhamland

Lady Louisa Anne Aylmer was the wife of General the Right Honourable Matthew Whitworth, 5th Lord Aylmer. He served in the Napoleonic Wars and the French Revolutionary Wars, and was appointed adjutant general of British forces in Ireland from 1814-1823.

To a quart of cold drawn linseed oil add a pint of vinegar, half an ounce of rose pink, four ounces of alkanite root and half an ounce of green Arabic dissolved. Put them all together in an earthen pan, let them stand three or four days, and it will be ready for use. Rub a small quantity over your table with a linen cloth and let it remain twenty four hours then rub it off with a different cloth and rub the table well with a clean one. This should be repeated very often or every time your table is dirtied or stained.

Parisian varnish for mahogany
Receipt for making varnish for furniture got at Paris 1815

Gomme laque is shellac, which is a resin secreted by the female lac bug, which is a scale insect, also known as kerria lacca, from India and Thailand. The bright red lac bug is from the same family of insects as the one from which cochineal is obtained. Copal is a type of tree resin, obtained mostly from trees in Africa and Brazil, which was considered very valuable for furniture polish.

Sandarac is a resin from the tetraclinis articulata tree from Africa. The resin oozes from the cut surface of the bark, and solidifies in the air to form 'sandarac tears', pale golden translucent flakes.

1 ounce of gomme laque, 1 ounce of copal, 2 ounces of sandarac
Boil all of these together in a pint of spirit of wine, with a low heat.

The furniture previous to being varnished must be polished very smooth with pumice stone and oil.

To clean marble or alabaster
From Lady Louisa Clements

Marble and alabaster should be kept free from dust, and should not come in contact with water. Alabaster is a fine grained form of gypsum, and is water soluble, so can be destroyed by water, so this recipe would be dangerous to use with alabaster. This remedy is practically identical to one given by Mrs Beeton in her famous book of housekeeping. Bullock's gall is the gall or bile of a bullock.

> ***A bullocks gall with a gill of turpentine and half a gill of soap lees mixed together with pipe clay to the consistence of thick paste. Apply it till you see the marble or alabaster clean and perfectly clear. If it does not succeed the first time it must be applied again. Then wash it off with a brush or sponge with cold spring water.***

From Ld Sydney's gardener, Frognal
To grow mushrooms in winter without the assistance of fireheat

Lord Sydney was John Townsend, 1st Earl Sydney, the son of John Townsend, 2nd Viscount Sydney, and his wife, Caroline Elizabeth Letitia Clements, daughter of Robert Clements and aunt to Nathaniel. He was a British liberal politician.
Text accompanying this caricature in Vanity Fair states:

A great hardship is that which is often inflicted on unoffending peers by exacting party leaders, who require them, as the price of official position, which should be theirs by right, to talk as if they understood political questions…it is fortunate for the Liberals that they are able to provide for so eminent a partisan as Lord Sydney the highly appropriate post of Chamberlain…the rights of women, as they are, lie in his absolute control - and the power that control gives is appalling… Lord Sydney has been at least equally successful in defining moral and material limits from the one extremity in vogue on the stage to the other which is affected in the palace.… Probably Lord Sydney's politics are liberal; possibly there are some ladies who think that his opinions are not liberal; but these are trifles. When his career is recorded, impartial history will write of him: "He received the Royal commands and lengthened the skirts of the ballet."

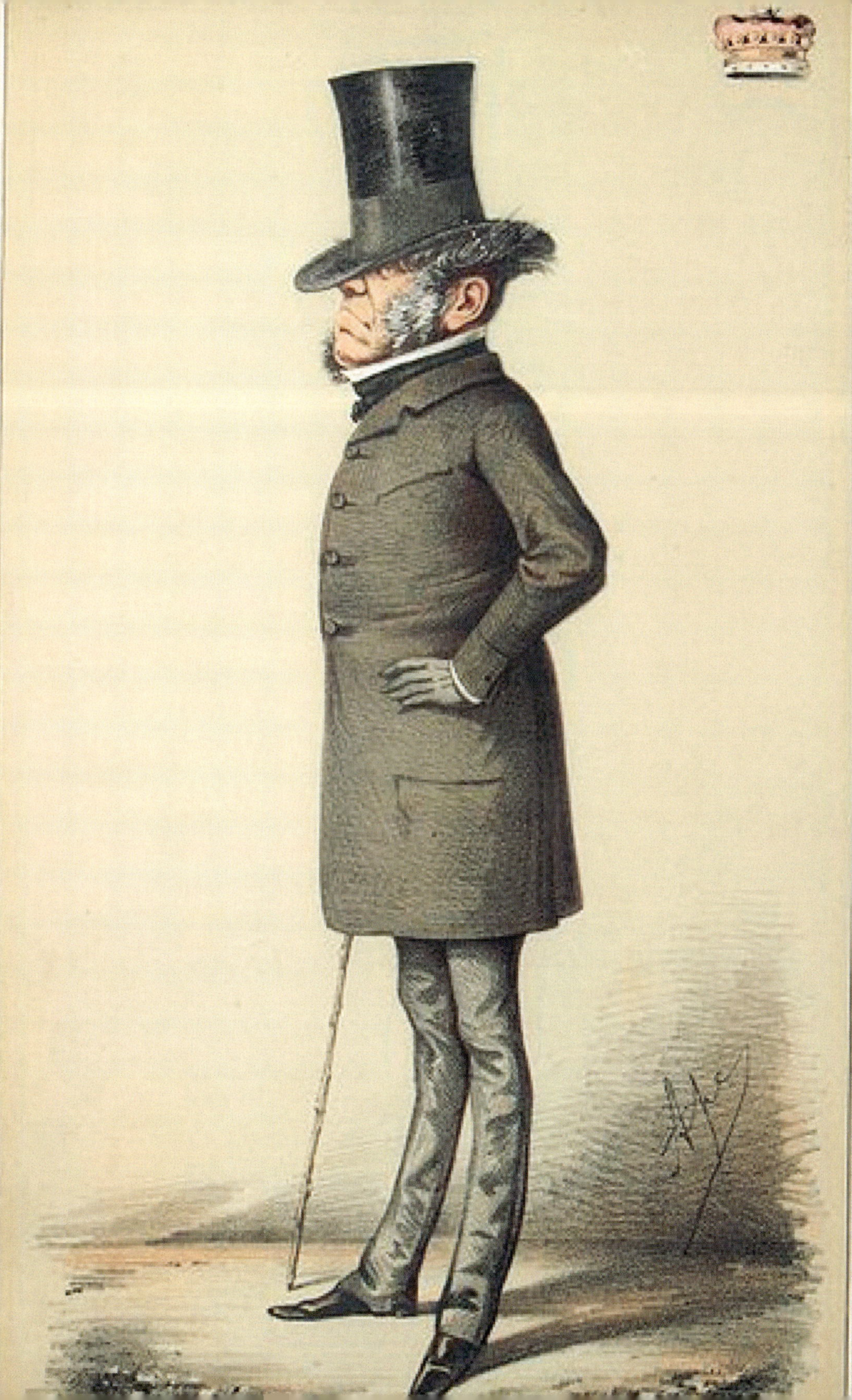

He lived with his wife in Frognal House in Foot's Cray, near Sidcup, in Greater London.

Prepare a proper quantity of dung by throwing it together for eight or ten days, turning it two or three times in the above time, then the dung is considered sufficiently heated. Begin by siting of a bed four and a half feet wide, by any given length, then a space of three foot wide for the lining, and another bed of four and a half feet wide, the inside of the beds next to the lining are to be carried up perpendicular 4½ or five feet high, the other sides to be sloping from the ground upwards.

When the beds are finished put in some batch Sticks to ascertain when they are in a fit state to receive the spawn. This part of spawning requires great attention as to the heat of the bed, because in my opinion the success of the crop, in a great measure, depends on the proper temperature of the bed, for if it is over hot when spawned and earthed up the heat is then considerably increased by being confined with the earth, then the spawn will inevitably perish, therefore rather let the bed be cold than over hot.

Having spawned and earthed up the bed, shake a little dry litter over it, in three weeks or a month the mushrooms will begin to appear. At the same time the beds will have considerably decreased in heat and the mushrooms will come on very slowly, unless they have more heat.

Having a proper quantity of dry leaves or hot dung, fill the space between the beds with either of them, which in a few days will throw in a fresh heat to the beds. The mushrooms will now come on well. As the heat decreases turn the lining, add a little fresh leaves or dung which keeps the beds in a proper temperature, by making the beds, the lining bar, the advantage of working them both and by gathering the beds in turns a more regular supply is obtained.

By the above method mushrooms may be grown in the winter months when by the common mode they seldom succeed owing as I observed before by the beds getting so soon cold, and not having the advantage of using the heat when wanted. I have grown mushrooms for three years on the above plan and have never failed of success. The better plan for the beds, it to have two or three posts according to the length of the bed, and two rails, one at top, another in the middle, the better to support the beds and prevent them from falling in.

Lady Cloncurry's receipt for mahogany

One quart of best linseed oil, one pint of spirit of turpentine, to be boiled together on a low fire or hot hearth for twenty minutes (great care must be taken that it does not catch fire.) When cold, to be rubbed with old linen every day on the tables, and not to leave them while the least moisture remains, that is the great secret to rub the stuff well into the wood. A brush must never be used. After three months every other day will be sufficient to put on the composition.

An effectual method of destroying rats

This is a particularly nasty concoction, and it is hardly surprising that rats decided not to come back after one of their number had been smeared with it. Oil of vitriol is sulphuric acid, which is an oily, highly corrosive toxic liquid that causes severe burns to the skin. Of course turpentine is a powerful solvent, distilled from pine resin. Oil of turpentine, as well as being a powerful irritant, would have caused tumors and ultimately death when applied to the rats' skin.

At a trap, take one alive. Smear him over with a composition of oil of vitriol and oil of turpentine. Turn him into his usual haunts and no more rats will be seen. This method has been tried and the premises have been cleared of these vermin for upwards of two or three years.

For young orange trees
J Knight, King's Road, Chelsea

Joseph Knight was a famous horticulturalist who opened his Exotic Nursery in Chelsea in 1808. His extraordinary nursery sold many unusual and rare shrubs and trees, with pineapples and fuchias among his early specialities.

In the 1830s he was sponsoring plant collectors to obtain new specimens from all over the world.

The water we apply to our young orange trees through the summer months is prepared as follows. To 40 gallons of common water mix one bushel of pigeon's dung, which stir up frequently. After standing three days take one quart of this infusion, which mix with one gallon of soft water for watering the trees.

Notice for cleaning Alabaster

After having taken off the dust with a brush, take some white vinegar and rub it well with another proportioned brush not so hard nor so softly for fear to break the small ornaments. After wash it in the same manner in fine clean fresh water, and immediately put in to the sun to dry. You shall see the alabaster fine and white, the same as new.

Receipt for a French polish for beautifying wood

To one pint of spirits of wine add one half oz of gum shellac, one half oz of gum lac, one forth oz of gum sandarac.
Place it on a gentle heat, frequently shaking it, till the gums are dissolved when it is fit for use. Make a roller of lint, put a little of the polish upon it, and cover that with a soft piece of linen rag, which must be slightly touched with cold drawn linseed oil.

Rub them in the wood in a circular direction, not covering too large a space at a time till the pores of the wood are sufficiently filled up. After this rub in the same manner spirits of wine, with a small portion of the polish added to it. A most brilliant polish will be produced if the article should have been previously polished with wax it will be necessary to clean it off with fine glass paper.

To fatten chickens
From Lady E Clements

One pound of rice boiled in a little skimmed milk will feed four chickens. That quantity is for one day and must be made fresh every day. 7 days is sufficient to fatten them.

Against Rats

Oil of Aniseed, or Oil of Anise is used to make the liquorice flavour in sweets. Rats are attracted to eat things that taste of it, as indeed are dogs. Pure rhodium is a metal, and part of the palladium group. A chemical complex of rhodium, rhodium chloride, is poisonous to rats. The powder of musk and the sugar in this recipe would attract rats.

Six ounces of sugar.
About half a doz of potatoes well pounded. 5 or 6 ounces of kitchen stuff, or pigs-grease. Half an ounce of white arsenic.
Put all into an earthen dish with:
6 drops of the oil of annice seed
6 drops of oil of thyme
3 drops of oil of lavender
3 drops of oil of rhodium
3 or 4 grains of powder of musk.

For the decoy.
Potatoes, sugar, flour and grease with a few of the above mentioned perfumes.

You will make up your decoy in small pieces equal to a marble, and throw them where you know rats frequent for 2 nights and by so doing where you find most of it eaten, you can put the most of the poison the third night.

Rat.

Chinese method of mending china

Flint glass was a type of glass manufactured from the 1820s, which had powdered flint added to the glass mixture to improve the glass clarity. In later years, the flint was replaced with lead, which made the glass heavier, with better clarity and reflective qualities.

> *Boil a piece of white flint glass in river water for five or six minutes, beat it to a fine powder, and grind it well with the white of an egg and it will join china without riveting, so that no art can break it again in the same place. Observe, the composition must be ground extremely fine on a painter's slab.*

To destroy bugs

Highly toxic corrosive sublimate is mercuric chloride. It's highly poisonous nature lead to many cases of mercury poisoning.

> *One ounce of corrosive sublimate, dissolved in a quart of spirits of wine.*

To destroy moths

Ladies in the 1800s wore tippets and muffs when they went outside. A tippet was a long scarf or wrap, often made of or edged with fur, and muffs were large cylinders of fur or fabric that ladies carried to warm their hands in.

The seed mentioned here is Abelmoschus moschatus, which is native to India. The unripe pods, leaves and new shoots are eaten as a vegetable, and the seeds smell sweet and musky. Oxymuriate of Mercury is a form of mercury which is poisonous, and was also used in a face cleanser in the regency period called Gowland's Lotion.

To destroy moths, or drive them from cloth, hairy tippets, muffs etc. The seed of the hibiscus abelmoschers (the vegetable muskseed) should be thinly distributed over the articles, and between the folds of cloth.

These seeds are highly esteemed by the French perfumers for their particularly delicate fragrance.

To destroy the vitality of the eggs, which produce the moths, deposited in woollen cloth, a weak solution of the Oxymuriate of mercury in spirit of rosemary (about ½ a drachm to a pint) or weak solution of the arseniate of Potass in the same spirit (about 15 grains to a pint) is employed by those who prepare the skins of birds and animals for stuffing.

ABOVE:
MOTHS

ABOVE:
TIPPETS AND MUFFS

Lady Dungannon's recipe for Pot Pourri

As this recipe is a wetter mix for Pot pourri, it would definitely be pourri, or rotten by the end of the winter. This Lady Dungannon may be Lady Charlotte Hill-Trevor, wife of Arthur Hill-Trevor, 2nd Viscount Dungannon.

Take Rose Leaves, Lavender, Bay leaves, Orange flowers, Clove and common pinks, in fact every flower except sweet pea.
Gather them in dry weather but do not suffer them to get quite dry before they put into the jar.
Add a large quantity of cloves, allspice, sweet pepper, peelings of oranges and lemons,
1 lb of bay salt, pounded fine.
The same quantity of common salt.
Strew this mixture over the flowers and let it and the flowers by placed in a jar in alternate layers, and then well stirred up together.
You may add flowers whenever you please, taking care to stir the mixture when you do so, and to add some fresh spices, salt etc. When the flower season is over, pour a pint of good lavender water into a large jar and wet it all, now and then, in the winter, with good brandy.

PINKS

Recipe for a dry pot pouri

Bay salt is a type of large crystalline salt made from the evaporation of sea water in salt flats or wide shallow pits. Storax is the resin of the Liquidambar orientalis tree, which is also called the oriental sweetgum. It was used as a fixative for scent.

To be made of rose leaves only which must be gathered in dry weather. Put them into a large pan and sprinkle over them pounded bay salt and common salt, laying the leaves and salt in alternate layers.

The powder to mix with them when the leaves are moderately dry, is composed of allspice, cloves, storax, benzoin, nutmegs and orris root powder, one ounce of each.

French polishing varnish upon mahogany furniture from William Hand
A copy of the French polishing varnish spreader. Killadoon, the 11th of May 1833

The furniture is to be well rubbed with soft linen cloths, so as to keep the damp and candle drops off the furniture. Then take a small piece of linen, wet it with the polish, rub the furniture with the grain of the wood and it will dry immediately and give a gloss to the wood.

How to revive gilt frames

Beat up three ounces of whites of eggs with one ounce of chloride of potassic or soda and do over the frame with a soft brush dipped in this mixture. The gilding will become immediately bright and fresh.

A grey wash for the walls of a room – Lady Elizabeth Clements

Four pounds of blue vitriol, two pounds of whiting to be washed in a well seasoned earthen pan for three hours, stirring it constantly, then let it stand till quite cold. Pour it off clear, and mix it with a sufficient quantity of size, to wash the room over as you do common white wash.

N.B. It keeps forever, before you mix it with size, therefore, you may prepare any quantity you please, and only add the size when you are going to use it. The above quantity is sufficient to wash a room 20 feet square four times over, as it should be done.

N.B. Blue Vitriol is from nine pence to a shilling a lb, and whiting about one penny per lb.

Diuretick Horse Balls
For bringing them into good condition

What exactly horse turpentine is in the following recipe is unclear. Turpentine was often used as a laxative and diuretic for horses in the nineteenth century. The 'balls' were usually two to three inch long cylinders, formed by hand. The use of these horse balls would be dangerous today.

12 oz of horse turpentine will make six balls. It is to be boiled in water for half an hour at least, then throw off the water and divide it. The horse is to get one of the balls every 4th day until he has taken three. Let the Ball be just softened in warm ale before it is given to the horse and drench him with the ale after. He is to fast two hours before and two after. Give him plenty of white water, walk him about.
If the turpentine stick to the hands, when it is making into balls, tis a sign that tis not boiled enough.

To cure lameness in a horses shoulder

Take 1 drachm of the oil of turpentine
½ a drachm of the oil of vitriol
1 drachm of the oil of amber
1 oz of the ointment of marshmallows
1 oz of nerve ointment

Marshmallow ointment, or Unguentum Althaeae, is made from the leaves of the marshmallow plant, or Althaea. The ointment was prepared by heating an equal amount of marshmallow leaves and lard, and straining, and was supposed to have a soothing, curative effect for all manner of strains.

All these to the mixed together and rubbed hard into the horses shoulder, holding a hot iron before it, to make it penetrate. Apply this once in two days for a week, and then every third day.

To take out paint from clothes

Take some brushwood and burn it and with the ashes of it mix the yolk of an egg. Rub that well on the place that has been stained with paint till it is in a lather, then wash it off with warm water.

Receipt – Rosemary for the hair

Rosemary has a reputation for stimulating hair growth, when made into a tonic for the hair, and also to add shine and lights to dark hair. It has been claimed that rosemary makes the hair grow stronger and more abundantly, and clears flakes from the scalp. Many people think that used regularly, it will cover grey hair too. This recipe is still commonly in use today as a hair rinse - without the rum!

Take a good handful of rosemary. Boil it in 2 quarts of water. Boil it well. Reduce it to one pint, then strain it into a jug. Let it get cold. Add half a pint of rum to it.

Receipt for pomatum

Early pomades were made from bears grease, but ox or cow marrow was easier to obtain, and overtook bears grease as the main component in pomade in the early 1800s. By the middle of the century, beef pomade was manufactured by many manufacturers in both Europe and America, and sold in small pots with transfer printed images of cows atop. It promised everything from softening the hair, to increasing hair growth.

Preserve some beef marrow. Put it into cold water for 40 hours. Change the water 8 times, then take the marrow and squeeze it from the water. Put it into a small pot. Let it stand by the fire until it's all melted then strain it though muslin into another pot. When it gets cold beat it up well until it becomes quite soft. Add whatever perfume you please.

To destroy slugs

Take a small portion of fresh lime and pour on it some hot water – when quite dissolved, add water sufficient to make it pass thro' a fine rose of a watering pot.

In a flower garden this will be found a very good plan and a great acquisition by watering the edging of box, thrift etc with it, for wherever it penetrates it is sure to kill even in a rainy season.

The last drop of the liquor will cause immediate death but with lime only, they frequently leave a slimy matter behind and escape.

OPPOSITE:
A POMATUM POT LID.
THANKS TO RICKSBOTTLEROOM.COM FOR THE IMAGE.

Receipt for cleaning boot tops
Major Elphinstone's recipe, 1815

Major-General William George Keith Elphinstone was an officer in the British Army. He was the commander of the 33rd Regiment of Foot, which he led at the Battle of Waterloo in 1815, the same date as this recipe.

In 1842 Major-General Elphinstone was in charge of a combined British and Indian force of the British East India Company who were forced out of Kabul in Afghanistan by an uprising. They attempted to retreat to Jalalabad across the mountains, but were massacred by the Afghans. Only one man, assistant surgeon William Brydon, survived from a total number of 16,000 soldiers and camp followers. Major Elphinstone was taken hostage, and died a captive.

1 oz of acid of sugar in a quart of skim milk if light brown, and new milk if brown. Sponge the tops and wash it off with water, then polish them with flannel.

ABOVE:
JUGDELLUK, THE LAST STAND MADE BY GENERAL ELPHINSTONE'S ARMY IN THE CALAMITOUS RETREAT. PLATE 21 AFTER JAMES RATTRAY.
FREDERICK WILLIAM HULME, PUBLIC DOMAIN, VIA WIKIMEDIA COMMONS

Stone colour wash for buildings

The cousin, E.S., who sent this colour wash recipe is unknown. Umber is a natural dark brown clay pigment, also called raw umber. When burned, the colour deepens to Burnt Umber. Umber has been used as a pigment since prehistoric times.

To two pecks of fresh slacked lime add 1 peck of roman cement, 3 pounds of blue black, 5 pounds of Spanish umber (all finely powdered).

Mix them together with strong lime water for use. The walls to be well cleaned before the wash is laid on.

My dear Coz – I have taken the trouble to copy this out for you, so be grateful.

Yours affectionately, E.S.

Acknowledgements

Years ago, Killadoon was filled with all manner of important documents, all of which remained unsorted. The historical importance of these papers was only fully realised with the arrival of Dr Anthony Malcomson.

Without his hard work, writing any book about the Clements family, or Killadoon, would be frankly impossible. He dived straight in to a daunting mountain of documents and produced a comprehensive calendar of the archive. As an expert historian, he has not only sorted these papers but also analysed them and written extensively about the family. I am also lucky enough to call him a friend. So thanks to Anthony, without whom this book would never have been written.

Thanks also to Christopher Moore, for long ago discussions on paint colours and compositions. The Fabre Museum, ricksbottleroom.com, and others.

Finally, to Lady Mary, who so carefully transcribed each letter into the book of receipts, keeping the originals safely tucked inside. Her curiosity, art and beauty continue to inspire.

Printed in Poland
by Amazon Fulfillment
Poland Sp. z o.o., Wrocław
08 April 2021

55db3523-8e8c-4f6a-ac4b-ae9abbb6e5bbR01